CRYSTAL HEALING BIBLE

The Ultimate Guide to Gain Enlightenment and Awaken Your Energetic Potential with the Healing Powers of Crystals

Crystal Lee

TABLE OF CONTENTS

INTRODUCTION

Hello, and welcome to my book, Crystal Healing Bible. In the chapters to follow, you will be learning the ultimate guide that will help you gain enlightenment and awaken your energetic potential with the healing powers of crystals. Whether you are new to healing crystals or have some practice, there is always something new to learn! I have filled this book with everything you need to know to get started with healing crystals. I hope that by the end, you feel at peace and secure with utilizing healing crystals to benefit your life.

In the first chapter, we will be going over the very basics of crystal healing. You will learn the basic concepts of crystal healing and how to get started. Along with this information, we will also be going over the power that crystals can hold and the vast history that has given us the power of the crystals. Once you understand this, we will delve into starting a collection of your very own!

Of course, you will know which crystals you will want to collect once you learn the incredible benefits of healing crystals. You will find how to heal different problems from addiction to increasing compassion, to finding happiness, patience, and even more. As you will learn, there are numerous benefits you can collect from healing crystals. You will learn a number of aspects from the configuration of the crystals, to the type of stone you can use whether it is the focus stone, intention stone, or perimeter stone.

In the third chapter, we will be going over your chakra connections and how crystals can help you heal and balance your chakras. If you have never studied chakras before, we will go over the basics, so you can begin to practice on your own. Chakras are the energy centers of your body. In Sanskrit, Chakra means "disk" or "wheel." You can think of these as spinning wheels of energy within your body. Our Chakras are in charge of keeping us functioning at optimal levels. You can use crystals to help heal these spots if you feel your energy is out of whack.

The fourth chapter will bring all of the information on some of the more popular crystals out there in the universe. You will be provided with information such as origin, shape, energy, color, placement, and use of each crystal. Knowing your crystals is going to be important, especially as you start your own collection. If you ever have any questions, feel free to refer back to this chapter so you can assure you are using the correct crystal in proper form.

Once you have learned some of the crystals and some of the amazing benefits, the fifth chapter will bring you even more uses for your crystals. You may be surprised to learn that you can use them for more than just health benefits! There are crystals for energizing your body, crystals that can be helpful for meditation, love stones if you lack in that department, and crystals to decorate and protect your home. As you will find out, crystals are incredibly versatile!

Finally, you will learn how to care for your crystals once you have started your own collection. This information will be vital when it comes to not only cleaning your collection but also recharging them. Much like our bodies, crystals can only do so much until they need a recharge. When your crystals are fully charged, you will be able to re-energize your own body and clear your mind of any negative energy. When you are ready to start your crystal journey, we can begin.

CHAPTER ONE

What Is Crystal Healing?

In the modern world, we seem to have an affinity with crystals and stones. They are found in our jewelry and our homes as sparkling decoration. What you may not realize is that the use of crystals dates back to the beginnings of our history. Crystals can be dated back to 60,000 years ago and are found in reference to both history and religion. Before we dive into the incredible benefits of the crystals, we will learn about its rich history, first.

Amulets

One of the first known usages of crystals were found in amulets. It is believed that some of the oldest amulets dated back to 30,000 years ago. The oldest amulets, the Baltic amber followed by amber beads, believed to be 10,000 years old. Other popular stones and crystals were jet beads discovered in Paleolithic gravesites in both Belgium and Switzerland.

It was in 335 AD that certain amulets were banned by Christian churches. Despite the ban, gem and crystals tend to have a role in all different types of religions. In the bible comes the first mention of birthstones. In the book of Exodus, there is a mention of the breastplate of Aaron, also known as the High Priest's Breastplate. On top of this, there is also the mention of stones and crystals in the Koran. One of the more popular examples comes from the Kalpa Tree. This tree is the representation of an offering to the Hindu Gods. It was thought to be made out of precious stones. In another example of a Buddhist text, there was thought to be a diamond throne near the Tree of Knowledge. As you can see, crystals are part of our religion's history, but they can also be found in other spots of our history, such as the Renaissance!

Renaissance

In school, you may have learned all about the Renaissance and all of the incredible advancements that came from that time period, but what you may not have learned about was the extensive use of crystals! In Europe, there were a number of medical treatises using precious and semi-precious stones used to treat certain ailments.

Typically, the stones were used hand-in-hand with herbal remedies.

On top of the healing ailments, stones were also thought to have qualities of protection and strength. One example of this comes from a chief justiciar in 1232 known as Hubert de Burgh. He was accused of stealing gems from King Henry III. It was believed that whoever wore these stolen stones would be invincible. He ended up giving these stones to King Henry's enemy, Llewellyn, who was the King of Whales.

These stones were thought to be corrupted by the sins of Adam, meaning the stones were inhabited by demons. With this state of mind, gems and crystals were always sanctified and consecrated before anyone was able to wear the crystals. This is why we cleanse and program our crystals in the modern world before performing any crystal healing. You will learn in our final chapter how you can perform a cleanse yourself, so you can avoid any problems.

The Beginning of Crystal Healing

The start of crystal healing can be dated back to 1609. The first person to suggest the virtue of gemstones comes from Anselmus de Boot who was a court physician in Germany. He suggested that the gemstones have a virtue due to the good and bad angels. Boot believed that good angels were able to grace certain gems, but on the other hand, bad angels were able to tempt humans to believe the stone itself as opposed to God's gift that was bestowed upon it. It wasn't until later in history that a man named Thomas Nichols introduced the concept of "Faithful Lapidary," meaning that inanimate objects could not possess effects from the past. During the Age of Enlightenment, precious stones were used more than ever to help with protection and healing.

What are Crystals?

You know that crystals can help with ailments, but what are crystals exactly? Crystals are natural elements that are created right here on earth. A true crystal has a lattice pattern known as a crystal system. As of now, six different lattice patterns have been found in healing crystals.

1. Hexagonal

Hexagonal crystals look much like a 3D hexagon. Typically, these crystals are used to help with manifestation.

2. Isometric

Isometric crystals have a cubic structure on their interior. These crystals are used to amplify energies and can help improve certain situations.

3. Monoclinic

Monoclinic crystals have a 3D parallelogram shape. For the most part, these crystals are used for protection.

4. Orthorhombic

Orthorhombic crystals are shaped like diamonds. These Orthorhombic crystals are used to help remove blockages, clean, and also clear any negative energy.

5. Tetragonal

Tetragonal crystals have an interior structure that is rectangular. These tetragonal crystals are used to make things more attractive and can help attract certain things to the wearer.

6. Triclinic

Finally, we have the Triclinic crystals. These crystals have three inclined axes. Typically, the triclinic crystals are helpful to ward off energies that are unwanted and are able to retain positive energies.

Another way we determine crystals are their different colors! As you may already realize, the color of the crystal can change how attracted you are to certain crystals. What you may not realize is that the color of crystals has a major role in the healing impact of crystals and their energy. You will learn later in the book how the color changes the healing powers of the crystals and which will be the best for your use.

Three different aspects create the color of the crystal. First, the color will change depending on how the crystal is able to absorb light. The color is also affected depending on the certain chemicals and minerals that are within the crystal. Another factor that can change the color of the crystal is any impurities it may have. The minerals and impurities impact the wavelengths of light that the crystal absorbs. One example of this would be a crystal that is able to absorb the entire light wavelength. Can you guess what color it will be? Black! The opposite is true for a crystal that is unable to absorb any light wavelength. If this happens, the crystal appears to be clear!

With the growing popularity of crystals and gemstones, there has been an increase in laboratory-created gemstones. For the most part, these crystals and gemstones are used in cheap jewelry. You can tell when a gem is made in the laboratory because it will be much less expensive compared to crystals that have been naturally formed.

Crystals that are formed within the earth can take millions of years to be created. This is why these crystals are thought to have strong, energetic power. While lab-made crystals still carry power and have the ability to retain energy, they are less pure. You will learn later how to sense energy from various crystals and how to feel the energy you need at any given moment.

Using Crystal Terms

If you research crystals, there seem to be several different terms such as rock, mineral, gems, and crystals. Most of the time, people use these terms interchangeably. It is important to realize that certain substances aren't crystals. To avoid confusion, here is a quick overview on which each term is:

1. **Crystal**

   As you already learned, crystals are a mineral that has a crystalline interior structure.

2. **Gem**

   A gem, on the other hand, is a crystal, mineral, or rock that has been cut and polished. An example of this could be a cut diamond. This cut diamond is a mineral, crystal, and rock. These minerals can be referred to as gems or gemstones. Other substances that are considered gemstones are amber and pearls, but they are not crystals, rocks, or minerals. You can probably see where the confusion comes from.

3. **Mineral**

   A mineral is a naturally-occurring substance. These minerals have a specific chemical composition and an ordered structure that isn't always crystalline. An example of this would be Opal. Opal is a gemstone and a rock but does not have a crystalline structure.

4. **Rock**

   A rock is a combination of minerals. One example of this is Marble. Marble is made up of several minerals and is a metamorphic rock. Metamorphic rocks are rocks that are subjected to pressure and heat over a certain amount of time.

Crystal Energy

Everything in our vast world has energy. Crystals have energy, and so does your body. You may not even understand your own energy at the moment, but over time, you will learn more. Imagine you are out with a group of friends and you get a bad feeling from a certain person, you just don't vibe with them and you don't quite understand why. When we experience this dislike for certain people, you are sensing their energy, and it simply isn't compatible with your energy.

This energy is the same for those negative and positive people in your lives. Have you ever been around a negative person and felt your mood take a dive? Your energy is being drained due to their negative energy. The same can be said for the energy of a positive person. Typically, the positive energy of this individual can help re-energize your energy and enhance your mood.

Crystal and Electric Effect

Another neat aspect of crystals is their electrical effects. One of these effects is known as the piezoelectric effect. This effect occurs when nonconducting crystals are able to generate an electric charge when placed under mechanical stress. One of the more popular crystals that demonstrate this effect would be Quartz. This is why this crystal is used in watches, radios, and other digital circuits.

In fact, Quartz crystals have been used in our technology as far back as the late 1800s. These crystals were used in several pieces of equipment such as radio, watches, and sonar. The use of Quartz can be found in military radios used in World War II. The military used oscillators made of quartz to help control the frequency of their radio transmissions. While these oscillators were precise, they were unfortunately hard to mass-produce. These quartz oscillators were also popular in watches. The crystals were excellent in timekeeping and only required a tiny piece of quartz.

On top of this, crystals also have their own vibration. As you learn to work with crystals, you will begin to notice how they are able to change your mind, spirit, and body energies. With this change in vibration to the body, it is thought that the vibration within the crystal can change as well. Typically, crystals have higher vibrations compared to our body, which is why they are helpful with advancing the body in a more positive direction.

Feeling Crystal Energy

There are metaphysicians, energy healers, mystics, and psychic mediums who have dedicated hours of their lives to communicate with spirits, meditate, and feel the energy that surrounds them. As a beginner, you may not have the experience or the ability to sense energy just yet. There are several ways you can learn how to feel crystal energy but remember that you will need time and practice.

First, it is important that you are open to the experience. There are plenty of people out there that are skeptical that crystals can carry power. If you lack belief in the crystal healing power, you are blocking the energy from coming in your direction. With this, you will also need to set aside any preconceived notions about crystals you may already have. You can't walk into this with high expectations of healing yourself instantly. You will learn to understand that the universe has a plan for you. If you allow yourself to be in the moment with your crystal, you will understand what it is trying to do for you.

Everyone has a unique experience with crystals. As a beginner, you will want to start with a crystal that attracts you. Your very first crystal should be exciting, one that truly calls for you. This crystal will be used for healing work because it is most likely calling to you for a reason. Later, you will learn the many different crystals and their healing powers but always listen to your own energy.

You may be wondering how you will feel when you first hold a crystal. This sensation from the crystal will change depending on your energy and the energy of the crystal. When you first start, all you will need to do is observe how you feel. You will want to pay special attention to any thoughts that arise, emotions you feel, and physical sensations you feel. It will be vital that you allow these to occur without any blocking or judgment. As you start, keep an open mind and experience the shifting of vibration. For some people, this may be subtle, for others, it will be much more noticeable.

It is important to realize that not everyone will react the same way to the crystals. For some, they are able to feel certain crystals lift their energy to high levels. For others, they may not feel anything. This doesn't mean that the crystal isn't working. It just means that the energy levels are different! How you end up experiencing crystals will change depending on your needs, beliefs, and own perspectives.

Crystal Myths

As mentioned earlier, an important aspect of harnessing the healing power of crystals is to keep an open mind. Unfortunately, many myths around crystals can cause disbelief in the powers of the crystals. One strong example of this is believing that the healing power is all in your head. When you work with crystals, you are meant to get out of your head. You will want to focus on the sensation alone. Thanks to the power of the crystal, there is no need to explain or rationalize what is happening. If you do feel concerned about using crystals, those thoughts are only in your mind. Instead of being focused on why it won't work, allow yourself to experience the sensations that come from the crystals and rationalize about those feelings later.

Another popular myth that circulates around crystals is the thought that if they are able to help people, they can also harm them. You will learn later that your crystals vibrate the energy that entrains with your energy. One of the major factors of using healing crystals will be your mindset and intention. If you go into the situation expecting the crystal to harm you, this, of course, is possible. Your belief in the crystal will change your experience and outcome. In general, you will want to approach the healing crystal with the intention of shifting your vibration to more positive energy.

The third myth about crystals is the mindset that you need to be spiritual in order to use crystals. While this is helpful, it isn't necessary. Just about anyone can use crystals. All you will need is to have an open mindset and the desire to change your energy. Even those who aren't spiritual or new-age have the ability to experience the healing power of the crystal.

A final myth I will mention here is the thought that more expensive crystals are the most powerful. One of the most powerful crystals is Quartz. Typically, quartz is fairly common and can be inexpensive. When you are starting your crystal collection, the amount of money you spend will make no difference on how effective the crystals are — the only factor that truly matters for the crystals is your energy and mindset. Sometimes, the least expensive crystals will be the ones that give you what you need.

As a beginner, you may feel the need to know everything at once. You could spend months immersing yourself in information, but you will need hands-on experience. Of course, you will need to educate yourself to help guide your crystal healing journey but remember to pick up the crystal along the way. With that in mind, we will now dive into starting your own crystal collection. Remember to find the crystal that attracts you. When you do, you will want to wear it, hold it, or even place it in your pocket. The more you experience crystals, the easier it will become to sense their energy.

Starting a Collection

Now that you have learned some of the crystal basics, it is time to get started on the fun part; starting a crystal collection of your own! Some people have crystals everywhere in their house while others just carry a few crystals in their pocket. You don't necessarily need a plethora of crystals to have a collection. All you will need is one or two. The major goal of a crystal collection will be to select your crystals mindfully. As you go through this book, you will be guided to the crystals as long as you follow your intuition.

I believe that crystals choose you just as much as you choose the crystal. You will learn that some crystals will serve a temporary need, and others, you will give to benefit other people who need them more. As you collect, you will buy some crystals for their beauty and others for their healing benefits. Later in the book, we will be going over different crystals in detail to help you select the best one for your life.

Places to Shop for Crystals

The first suggested place to shop for crystals would be a crystal/metaphysical shops. When you are selecting crystals, you will want to hold them and feel their energy. Many cities and towns have crystal outlets. Most times, these stores are listed as New Age shops, crystal stores, or even metaphysical bookshops.

Another location to purchase crystals would be a crystal, mineral, and gem show. These are traveling shows for crystals and are great for buying crystals at good prices. It should be noted that you will most likely have to travel to these shows and pay an entry fee. If you see a show coming to your town, you will definitely want to plan a trip. At these shows, the dealers typically have a vast knowledge of crystals and will allow you to handle them before any purchase.

Finally, you can always find an online retailer for your crystals. There are different craft sites such as Amazon, Etsy, or eBay. This can be tricky as you cannot hold the crystal to feel their power. Instead, try checking out the seller feedback before buying any crystals and checking their overall rating. This way, you get a good vibe from the seller, and hopefully, good vibes from the crystals as well.

Understanding Crystal Shapes

When you first start purchasing crystals, you will find two basic categories for the crystal shape. It is natural and polished. In general, the natural stones, also known as raw or rough, will have more powerful energy. It should be noted that more power isn't always better. In the case for beginners, it is better to start with polished stones as they have subtler energy.

Rough Stones

One of the main factors of rough stones you will notice is that they look very much like they were just removed from the earth. Some of the raw stones you find may appear as though they have broken off into smaller stones. In general, rough stones maintain their natural form and have never had any human intervention. There are a few different rough stones as followed:

1. Blades
   Blades are rough stones that are exactly as they sound. These stones are typically long and flat. A blade stone has jagged areas and is best known as a worry stone. This stone is great to rub your thumb along the smooth area to help soothe any stress you may have.
2. Cluster
   A cluster rough stone contains a group of crystals. One of the more popular cluster stone would be a cluster of quartz. These stones are best for direct energy if it is needed in a specific area.

3. Geodes
   Geodes are rough stones that have open cavities in which are lined with crystals. Typically, this type of rough stone is used for decorating the house.

4. Point
   Point stones have one pointed end known as single-terminated or two pointed ends known as double-terminated. The stone will also have one flat end. A popular point stone is a smoky quartz. This rough stone is typically used to point direct energy toward something.

5. Rough Crystals
   Rough crystals often just look like rocks. These types of rough stones have no certain shape and can change size. Depending on the size of the stone, these crystals can help with a number of healing factors.

6. Wand
   As you could have guessed, a wand natural stone is long and narrow. The difference is, the stone isn't shaped deliberately. It appears naturally in the earth. A wand rough stone is also an excellent choice for a worry stone.

Cut and Polished Stones

While rough stones look the way they sound, cut and polished stones are glossy and smooth. While some still have their natural shape, other crystals can be cut into a specific shape. As you will learn, different shapes hold different properties. When you work with this type of crystal, the shape of the crystal is able to impart properties of both the sacred shape as well as the power of the crystal itself. Below, I will explain some of the more popular shapes to help you decide which would benefit you most.

1. Dodecahedron
   The Dodecahedron looks much like a circle with edges. This shape is mostly associated with an element known as Ethers. It is thought that this shape helps connect individuals to their intuition and higher realms.

2. Hexahedron
   A hexahedron is also known as a cube. This shape is known to represent the element of earth. For most people, this shape helps with grounding and stability.

3. Icosahedron
   An Icosahedron is mostly known for its link to the element of water. This shape helps people connect to the way they change and flow in any given situation.

4. Octahedron
   An Octahedron looks like two triangles placed together. This shape is best known to represent the element of air. For the holder, it promotes feelings of love, forgiveness, kindness, and compassion.

5. Sphere
   A sphere crystal looks much like a marble. It is thought that this shape holds energy that helps people feel whole, complete, and one with the world.

6. Tetrahedron
   A tetrahedron is the shape of a triangle or pyramid. This crystal shape is best represented with the element of fire. This crystal helps the holder promote stability, balance, and introduces the ability to create change.

7. Merkaba
   A Merkaba is the shape of a 3D star. This shape contains all of the elements of those above and combines them so that the holder can experience the effects of each element. Mostly, this crystal shape is associated with eternal wisdom and sacred truth.

Choosing your Crystals

If you are a true beginner with crystals, you may have absolutely no idea where to start. While of course in the third chapter, we will be going over many different crystals, there are ten crystals that make for an excellent starter kit. These crystals are known as crystal workhorses and are crystals that absolutely everyone should have. Of course, these crystals are just a suggestion, but you can always add on and use these as a jumping off point.

1. Clear Quartz

Any crystal collector should have clear quartz in their collection. Clear quartz is a great crystal to have as the crystal is able to work with every type of energy.

2. Citrine

Citrine is an excellent crystal to have for any beginner as it is able to help promote both prosperity as well as self-esteem.

3. Smoky Quartz

You will learn later in this book that smoky quartz is a manifestation stone. This stone is able to convert any negative energy into more positive energy.

4. Turquoise

While also beautiful, turquoise stones have the ability to promote personal power, prosperity, as well as luck.

5. Rose Quartz

If you are seeking love in your life, rose quartz will be vital for your collection. This stone is able to support all different types of love such as romantic love or even unconditional love.

6. Hematite

Hematite is a stone that is used to attract energies into your life. It is also associated with centering and grounding and is a protective stone.

7. Amethyst

If you are looking to tune guidance and intuition into your life, amethyst will be good to add to your first collection. This stone also has the power to help with your dreams.

8. Carnelian

Are you looking to become a more creative individual? Carnelian will be essential for your crystal collection. This stone is able to help with integrity and also allows individuals to set appropriate boundaries for themselves.

9. Black Tourmaline

As a crystal collector, you will need a protector. Black tourmaline is great for this and can also help keep negative energies at bay if that is something you typically experience.

10. Rainbow Fluorite
    Finally, we have rainbow fluorite. This crystal is best known to promote love, facilitate clear communication, and also has the ability to deepen intuition.

As I said, these are mere suggestions. In the third chapter, you will have a better understanding of crystals for your own needs and collection. You will want to choose crystals based on their system. Later in this book, we will explain the different crystal systems and how they each have certain properties. Some of these crystal systems include:

1. Triclinic Crystals
   These ward off energies

2. Tetragonal Crystals
   These attract energies

3. Orthorhombic Crystals
   These clear, unblock, and release energies

4. Monoclinic Crystals
   These crystals help protect you

5. Isometric Crystals
   These crystals can help amplify energy and improve situations

6. Hexagonal Crystals
   These have the ability to manifest

Another way people choose their crystals is by their color. As you will learn, each crystal's color will have vibrational energy that is connected to their healing property. Later in this book, we will be going over the different colors and their specific property. By having this knowledge, you will be able to select your crystals for certain conditions.

Finally, you will want to choose your crystal based on how they make you feel. Crystal selection relies heavily on intuition. This is why I suggest you hold the crystals in your hand and let them tell you how they make you feel. In hand, you will instantly be able to tell if a crystal makes you feel comfortable or not. You will want to feel a pleasing sensation before you buy, if not, it isn't the right crystal! You will always want to pay attention to the attraction you feel toward any crystal as they are most likely calling to you for a reason.

Tips and Tricks for Crystal Shopping

1. Ground Yourself

   As a crystal beginner, you may feel a bit disoriented when you enter a crystal shop. The energy of the store itself can seem overwhelming, which is why you will want to ground yourself before entering the shop. You can do this by closing your eyes and visualizing your roots growing from your feet and into the earth. If you still feel lightheaded in the shop, try picking up a black stone to help ground you.

2. Follow your Intuition

   This is vital when shopping in a crystal store. You will more than likely be drawn to a certain location. It is the crystal calling to you. Remember, always to follow your intuition as it is happening for a reason.

3. Ask Away

   If you walk into a shop or gem store, you will most likely find an expert in the crystal department. If you have any questions on finding the right crystal, never be afraid to ask. Asking questions is also a wonderful way to educate yourself. On top of asking questions, feel free to reference this book!

4. Don't Jump

   If you are just starting your collection, it is easy to get overwhelmed, especially by shiny objects. You should never just grab the first pretty stone you see. Instead, shop around and see which stones are calling to you. Once you have selected your stone, you will want to compare prices and find the best price for the crystal you want.

5. Reputation of Seller
    Before you stop into a store, you will want to check out the reputation of the seller. Unfortunately, there are scammers out there who are just looking to make a buck. Take to the internet to search for reviews before you hand over your hard-earned cash to just any person selling crystals.

6. Touch
    Any true crystal seller will allow you to hold the crystals before you purchase them. It is important that you handle the crystal to see how they make you feel. You will instantly sense the energy coming from the crystal to see if it is calling out to you or not. If the owner of the shop says no touching, walk out. Most likely, this person doesn't really understand how healing crystals work.

Power of Crystals

While collecting crystals is one part of the journey, the other part is to understand the healing powers of each crystal. One of the major reasons that healing crystals work is due to the energy you feel when you hold them in your hand. They are concrete examples that help individuals move to other modalities when they become more comfortable with crystals. Eventually, you will be able to move to chakra work, sound practice, meditation, mantras, and even more. At the end of the day, you will practice healing practices that resonate most with you. One major way you can further your practice with crystal is learning how to use crystals in conjunction with other crystals. This is known as a crystal grid. A crystal grid is when you combine crystals based on their sacred geometry. By doing this, you will be able to grow the energy of the crystals to be more focused and much more powerful. A grid can be simple or complex depending on how comfortable you are with crystals. In order to use a grid, you can place them anywhere whether it is on your bed or even on your disk. Below, I will go over some grid shape examples to help you get started.

1. Spirals
   A spiral grid is used to represent a path to consciousness.

2. Circles
   If you use a circle grid, this is perfect to represent unity and oneness.

3. Vesica Piscis
   This grid is two circles that combine. This is helpful if you are trying to represent creation.

4. Squares
   A square grid represents the earth's elements.

5. Triangles
   If you create a triangle grid with your crystals, this helps create a connection between the mind, body, and the spirit.

On top of the placement, the grid arrangement will also be important. Your grid will need to follow certain elements for it to work. To start, you will want to place your focus stone in the center of the grid. You can think of this as the stone that holds the primary energy you would like to achieve. Once in place, you will place the appropriate surrounding stones to help amplify the energy. By doing this, you allow the energy to flow outward from the focus point.

If you desire, you can also place outer stones around the surrounding stones, though this isn't required. Outer stones are often placed to be a source of intention for the primary energy you are trying to achieve. These stones can also be a perimeter stone if you wish to keep the intentional energy within your grid.

One example of a grid arrangement would be a grid for creativity. The configuration you will want to use is the Vesica Piscis. As you will recall, this looks like two circles that are intertwined. To achieve the most creativity, you will want to place the citrine as your focus stones, surrounded by amethyst for your perimeter stone.

Another example of a grid arrangement will be if you are seeking forgiveness, whether it is for yourself or from another person. The configuration you would use would be a spiral. Start by placing your focus stone, selenite, in the center. Going out from this stone, you would want to use clear quartz points to amplify the energy through the perimeter stones. As you learn more about crystals, you will be able to put your own grids together eventually.

Now that you understand the basics of crystals, it is time to understand the health benefits that come from the crystals. As you go through the different benefits such as help for addiction, increased happiness, or creating patience, take mental notes on what you wish to improve in your life. By thoroughly understanding the healing powers of crystals, you will have a thorough understanding of which crystals you will need to introduce into your life.

CHAPTER TWO

Health Benefits Of Crystal Healing

As you work more with crystals, you will learn different strategies that work for you. The following information in this chapter is mere suggestions. The more you work with crystals, the more you will be able to choose crystals that work best for you. What you will need to remember is that healing will take some time. In order to make any changes, you must have an open heart and an open mind.

Being a beginner, you will need to learn how to set aside any doubts or fears you may have about crystals. Instead, enter your practice with a receptive and positive mindset to help with your healing. You can only heal if you are willing to receive the powers of the healing crystals. Due to this, I will grace you with a mantra to start each session with. In the chapter to follow, you will find a mantra for the problem, followed by two healing stones that can be used, and a grid that may be helpful with your practice. You can start with these suggestions, and then come up with some solutions of your own as you learn more about crystals.

Addiction

Many people struggle with addiction. While some people have an addiction to alcohol or drugs, other people have an addiction to unhealthy relationships and unhealthy diets. No matter what you are addicted to, you can often feel helpless in any given situation. Luckily, there are some remedies you can try to help you release from any unhealthy attachments you have and gain the strength to free yourself from any given addiction.

Mantra:

I have an addiction. I choose to release this unhealthy attachment. I will move forward and release myself from this addiction

Healing Stone:

1. **Hematite**
   In the chapter to follow, you will be learning more about your chakras. It is thought that most addictions stem

from our root chakra. In this case, you will want to use a crystal that can help bring balance to this chakra. Hematite is a crystal that is able to absorb energy to help take away any power an addiction may hold over you.

One way to use the hematite is to place it beneath a place you sit through the day. Some examples of this could be on your bed or your chair at work. You can also carry the crystal with you, so it is with you through the day. For those moments when you feel the addiction urges wash over you, simply hold the hematite in your dominant hand and repeat the mantra until the addiction urge passes. Remember to cleanse the hematite after using it all day. We will be going over the cleansing process in the final chapter.

2. Amethyst

This crystal is often referred to as the sobriety stone. It is thought to help protect individuals from becoming drunk. If you are an individual who is addicted to any substance that alters your mind such as alcohol, caffeine, or even nicotine, amethyst will be beneficial for you. To use this crystal, you will just need to carry it in your pocket. When your addiction urges strike, place the crystal in your dominant hand and repeat the mantra until you feel better.

Healing Grid

As mentioned, addiction can be related to your root chakra. The healing grid you will want to create with your healing crystals is going to be a basic layout of chakra stones. You will want to create this grid in a location where you typically spend most of your time. We suggest placing it on your bed or on your desk. Each one of the crystals will absorb your chakras from any excess energy that may be causing your addiction.

Configuration: Vertical Line

Stones Needed:

- Howlite (Crown)

- Lapis Lazuli (Third-Eye)
- Sodalite (Throat)
- Malachite (Heart)
- Yellow Tigers Eye (Solar Plexus)
- Carnelian (Sacral)
- Black Tourmaline (Root)

Anger

Anger. It is an emotion that we all experience from time to time. We get angry when we are stuck in traffic and are late to work. We get angry when our loved one doesn't listen to what we say. We even get angry when our food gets burned! It is so easy to get angry about things that are out of our control. This emotion can become debilitating when you suffer from long-term anger. Sometimes, these emotions can come out as resentment, frustration, or even rage. When you start working with healing crystals, the powers can help you release some of this anger, so you can move forward with your life.

Mantra:

At this moment, I am feeling anger. I have the power to control my anger. I will choose to be calm and positive.

Healing Stones:

1. **Malachite**

   It is believed that anger is linked to our heart chakra. Anger is an emotion of excess energy and over-expression. This emotion can be absorbed by an opaque crystal. This crystal is able to absorb the energy as you release it. The malachite crystal is a deep green color and holds the ability to absorb any excess energy you are releasing. If anger and rage are emotions you experience daily, try wearing the malachite on a long cord so that it lies over your heart. In the case that wearing the crystal doesn't work, place the crystal in your hand and repeat the mantra until the feelings pass you by.

2. **Black and Red Jasper**

23

For some people, anger happens when they are afraid. Anger is a defense mechanism that can protect you from feeling afraid. If this resonates with you, you could benefit from a red or black opaque stone such as Jasper. This stone can help you by just simply carrying it in your pocket. In the chance that you are feeling afraid and angry, simply place the stone into your hand and plant your feet to the floor. Close your eyes and visualize a cloud draining through your feet and repeat the mantra until you feel more secure.

Healing Grid:

When it comes to anger release, a circular grid will be most helpful. As you already learned, a circle grid stands for unity and oneness. As you place your stones, they will amplify compassion as well as absorb any anger you are feeling. You will want to place this grid under your bed or anywhere you spend a lot of time.

Configuration: Circle

Stones Needed:

- Malachite (Focus Stone)
- Rose Quartz (Intention Stones)

Balance

It should come as no surprise that balance is vital in our lives. When we feel out of control, we feel unbalanced and unhappy. Unfortunately, a lack of balance in certain areas can lead to a lack of balance in other parts of your life like work, love, and friendship. The very first step you will need to take is to recognize that you are out of balance in the first place. Once you have come to terms, you can use some crystals to help you find your balance again.

Mantra:

I have the power to balance myself. I am balanced and at peace.

Healing Stones:

1. Rainbow Fluorite

You will be learning in the next chapter that rainbow fluorite has a wide array of colors. Thanks to the colors, this crystal is able to help balance energies. The crystal is also so beautiful. It is perfect to wear as jewelry to bring you to balance through the day. If at any point, you begin to feel imbalanced, all you will need to do is place it in your non-dominant hand a repeat your mantra.

2. Turquoise

This stone is often known as the stone of harmony. By wearing turquoise in your jewelry, it can help balance your energy so that you can bring peace back to your life.

Healing Grid:

The healing grid to find your balance is a bit different. You will need black tourmaline and clear quartz for this healing grid. What you will need to do is find a comfortable place in your home and lie down. I suggest your bed or even the sofa. Once in place, you will place the black tourmaline on your root chakra and the quartz near your crown chakra. If you have no idea where these are, we go further into your chakras in the next chapter. After, you will close your eyes and imagine your energy flowing from each chakra. As you do this, repeat your mantra until you feel balanced.

Compassion

Compassion is an important quality for just about anyone, but it is something that people often forget. We forget to have compassion for not only others but also for ourselves. Compassion can be difficult and frustrating, but it is necessary if you wish to experience yourself in a Divine manner. Several crystals can help you develop more compassion.

Mantra:

I have the ability to see everyone and everything with eyes of compassion. I am a compassionate and loving person.

Healing Stones:

1. Rose Quartz
As you probably already know, compassion is an emotion that comes not only from our hearts but also from our spirits. In order to experience an emotion such as compassion, you will want to choose a stone that amplifies the desire to nurture and grow compassion. Rose quartz is the perfect stone for this as it has one of the highest vibrations to cultivate compassion.

You can use rose quartz in a few different ways. If you are searching for self-compassion, you will want to hold the stone in your non-dominant hand, hold it at your heart, and repeat your mantra. If it is compassion for others you are searching for, place the stone in your dominant hand, hold at your heart, and repeat the mantra as many times as you need to.

2. Aquamarine
When it comes to compassion, it can be hard to experience unless you release any judgments you may be having about certain individuals. Aquamarine holds power to help you let go of these emotions. If you experience yourself being judgmental, all you will need to do is hold the stone in your dominant hand, close your eyes, and picture yourself releasing this emotion. You will want to repeat a mantra such as, "I will allow compassion for this person. I am choosing to release my judgment."

Healing Grid:

For this practice, you will need Peridot. Peridot, known as a heart stone, is best known for its quality of compassion. For this practice, you will need first to find a comfortable location. We suggest your bed or a nice, soft sofa. When you find this place, lie down on your back and place the peridot on your heart chakra. When you feel safe, close your eyes and notice the beating of your heart. As you focus on your breath, visualize a person who you have compassion for. Notice your emotions and sensations for this person and feel it through your whole body. Practice for as long as you need to help bring more compassion into your life.

Confidence

While there seems to be a bad reputation behind confidence, it is essential for life. It is important to realize that there is a very fine line between confidence and arrogance. If someone comes across too confident, people are turned off by this quality. When you are confident in yourself, it brings balance to your life to be successful and joyful. If you feel you are lacking in the self-confidence department, there are a few crystals that can help you out.

Mantra:

I love myself. I accept myself unconditionally. Being confident is okay.

Healing Stones:

1. **Yellow Tigers Eye**
   If you lack self-confidence, you may benefit from meditation with a yellow tiger's eye in hand. This stone helps absorb any negative energy you feel for yourself and can absorb excess confidence that makes people come across arrogant. While you meditate, hold the stone in your dominant hand and repeat your mantra to remind yourself that you will accept yourself for who you truly are.

2. **Citrine**
   Citrine is a stone that has the ability to amplify self-confidence. This is only useful if you recognize the confidence within yourself already. Of course, this will be something that you will need to practice. You can build your confidence and strengthen it by holding the stone in your non-dominant hand and meditate quietly.

You will want to visualize a golden light around you, flowing through the stone and into your body.

3. Amber

Finally, you can use amber to help build your confidence. Most of our confidence comes from our solar plexus chakra. Many people wear amber in their jewelry to help build their self-confidence when they need it most out in public. You can wear a necklace or bracelet as a visual reminder that it is okay to be confident.

Courage

When the lion was on his way to see the Wizard of Oz, he was going to ask for courage. What he found was that it was within him all along. Finding courage isn't always due to being afraid of something, it can be finding the courage to do what is best for you. If you ever find you need more courage in a trying situation, there are a few crystals that could help you on that path.

Mantra:

I have the courage within my mind and soul to do what is best for me.

Healing Stones:

1. Citrine

Citrine has a golden yellow color that is able to amplify the energy to your solar plexus. It is thought that courage arises from this chakra, so in times that you are looking for courage, this stone is excellent to create a power source. For it to work, you will hold the stone in your non-dominant hand and repeat the mantra from above.

2. Aquamarine

Another stone that represents courage is aquamarine. This stone is beautiful and looks great in jewelry. If you feel you need courage through your day, for any situation, you can wear this on a daily basis. For the moments you need an extra boost of courage, call to the stone and repeat your mantra for the courage.

Healing Grid:

The healing grid for courage is called a courage grid. You will want to place this grid in a location you spend a lot of time in. You will need the following stones to help amplify the energy.

Configuration: Square

Stones Needed:

- Amazonite (Focus Stone)
- Aquamarine (Intention Stone)
- Citrine (Intention Stone)
- Clear Quartz Points (Perimeter Stone)

Forgiveness

There is a lot of misunderstanding about what forgiveness can mean. For some, it is about letting go of anger or resentment to another person, but that isn't necessarily always true. Forgiveness truly happens when you let go of the pain that is caused by another's actions. You will also want to learn how to forgive yourself. Often, we are our own demise. It is important that you learn how to love yourself just as you love others. Crystals can help with all different types of forgiveness whether you need it for yourself, or a person you have had a struggling relationship with.

Mantra:

I am choosing to let go of the pain I have felt in the past. I will move forward with love, compassion, and forgiveness in my heart.

Healing Stones:

1. Apache Tears

Apache Tears are the perfect stones if you are looking to overcome any painful or difficult feelings you are experiencing. These stones grant the ability to let go of negative feelings so that you will be able to forgive and move forward with your life. For this stone to work, you will hold it in your dominant hand and close your eyes. As you find your breath, imagine there is a dark shadow floating from your heart, down your arm, and into the crystal. Once you feel clear from this negative energy, imagine telling the person or yourself, I forgive you.

2. Rhodochrosite

Rhodochrosite is a stone that is also able to help with forgiveness. This stone is a pink color that some people find themselves instantly attracted to. For this stone to work, all you will need to do is hold the stone over your heart using both hands. Once in place, close your eyes and repeat your mantra of forgiveness until you feel the pain leaving your body.

Healing Grid:

Earlier in the book, we described the forgiveness grid. Please feel free to go back to check out this grid before moving forward. When your grid is in place, you will just need to visualize the person you are seeking to forgive. Imagine that you are fixing the energy ties between the two of you and repeat your Mantra. Once you forgive the person, imagine a lovely and positive white energy that surrounds them.

Grief

Unfortunately, grief is a natural part of life. We experience this emotion when we lose something we love. Of course, it is vital that you allow yourself to experience this emotion fully in order to move past this moment. It does become an issue when you get stuck in this emotion. When we are stuck grieving, we often miss out on life's moment that is meant to be joyful. Luckily, working with crystals can help the grief pass in a healthy manner. With the use of crystals, you will be able to remove any blockages so that you can move forward with your life.

Mantra:

I will let go of this grief. I am filled with love and love will heal my pain.

Healing Stones:

1. **Apache Tears**

   Much like with forgiveness, this stone also works for grief. While the stone itself can't make the emotion go away, it will help you healthily process the emotion. If you are in the middle of grieving, try carrying the crystal with you to help process the emotion. It is helpful to place it next to your bed, so its energy is near you while you are sleeping.

2. **Ruby**

   When we are grieving, our hearts are wounded. Ruby is an excellent stone to help heal your heart. To use this stone, lie down with the ruby held gently to your heart chakra. You will want to repeat your mantra for grief and visualize a healing light enter your heart chakra, washing away any grief you are experiencing.

Healing Grid:

You will want to create a grief grid to help heal yourself. This is also known as a stages-of-grief grid. Much like with other grids, you will want to create it where you spend a lot of time. Each stone will represent a different stage of grief. You will notice that there is no true focus or perimeter stone. Instead, focus on each stone to help go through each stage of grief.

Configuration: Spiral

Stones Needed:

- Apache Tear (First Stone, Grief)
- Hematite (Anger)
- Rainbow Fluorite (Denial)

- Blue Kyanite (Bargaining)
- Smoky Quartz (Depression)
- Amethyst (Acceptance)

Happiness

While I think we all wish we could be happy all of the time, it is something we can easily lose sight of. We often become overwhelmed with our day-to-day lives and can get stressed out. Often, we can forget to experience happiness or joy. With the help of crystals, you will have a reminder to choose to be happy. It is okay to get stressed out; it is going to happen. It is important to let go and be happy!

Mantra:

At this moment, I choose to have happiness and joy.

Healing Stones:

1. **Amber**
   Amber is often associated with happiness. First, it has a gorgeous golden color that radiates natural warmth. Many people wear amber to help cultivate the energy of happiness. You can wear it as a visual reminder to be happy. It is something you can choose, no matter what the situation is. If you ever fall under the spell of stress, hold the amber in your non-dominant hand and repeat your mantra until you feel the happiness return to your soul.

2. **Smoky Quartz**
   Smoky quartz is a stone that is able to turn negative energy into positive energy. If you feel more stressed out than usual, you can take a moment to meditate with this stone in each hand. As you sit or lie down to meditate, close your eyes and visualize the negative energy flowing through you. Once you have it in your mind, imagine the energy flowing into each stone in your hands. The negative energy leaves your body and is replaced with warm, happy energy.

3. **Citrine**

Citrine is a stone that has the ability to spread joy and happiness. If you are going to a social situation but aren't in a good mood, try holding citrine before you leave. You will want to place it in your dominant hand and tell yourself; I will spread only happiness. Repeat this mantra until you believe it in your soul, and then pop the stone into your pocket. It will be your reminder to spread happiness to those who surround you.

Love

You are loved, even if you don't realize it. It is important to remember that not all love is a romantic love. However, when we lack this type of love, people often feel lonely. One of the most popular reasons people get into crystal healing is to help with love. With the help of crystals, you will be able to help with all different types of love in your life.

Mantra:

I choose to give love to others, and I receive this love in my heart and soul.

Healing Stones:

1. **Rose Quartz**
   Rose Quartz is the most widely used crystal for those seeking unconditional love in their life. Most people find this stone in a heart-shape. However, it isn't necessary for your use. If it is romantic love you are looking for, you will want to meditate with this stone held against your heart chakra. As you settle into your meditation, imagine a love energy coming from your heart, flowing to your crystal, and exploding into the universe. You can think of this stone as a magnet to attract love in your direction. As you meditate, remember to repeat your own mantra about love.

2. **Peridot**
   Difficulty in relationships can be taxing and frustrating. Whether this love is romantic or platonic, the peridot stone is an excellent source to help release any hurt feeling or anger you may be experiencing at the moment.

The peridot brings healing energy to you and your relationship when used during meditation. As you settle in, you will want to hold this stone against your heart chakra. Once in place, you will want to visualize the person you are having difficulty with. As you picture them, imagine a green light extending from your heart, through the stone, and to the heart of this individual. This light will heal your emotions and relationship as you repeat your mantra.

3. Pink Tourmaline

A final crystal that is known to help with the emotions with love is pink tourmaline. If you find yourself in a relationship where you lack trust, this is a major block for love. By using pink tourmaline, the crystal healing powers may help you build this trust toward another person. For this crystal to work, you will want to hold the stone in your dominant hand and visualize the energy surrounding you. You will feel the warmth and trust building up inside you. Repeat your mantra until you believe it in your heart and soul.

Motivation

Sometimes, motivation is hard to find. When we want to accomplish our dreams, it takes a lot of self-motivation. It is thought that motivation comes from our solar plexus. The solar plexus is in charge of our personal will which can experience imbalances of energy. When this happens, we can lack motivation. With the help of crystals, you can help restore and rebalance these energies to get you moving in a positive direction.

Mantra:

I choose to be motivated. I can do it, and I will be it.

Healing Stones:

1. Yellow Tigers Eye

Yellow Tigers Eye is a stone that can help you with your personal will. For this stone to work, you will want to begin meditation and place the stone against your solar plexus chakra. Once you do this, you will repeat your mantra until you believe it in your heart and soul. If you don't have time to meditate, place the stone in your hand, close your eyes, and state a mantra for the activity you are trying to gain motivation for. An example of this would be if you are trying to find the motivation to eat healthily. Try saying, I choose to consume foods that support my health. You will want to repeat this until you believe it.

2. **Rainbow Fluorite**
   Rainbow Fluorite is a stone that is commonly known to help with both motivated and keeping individuals focused. If you are a person who lacks motivation constantly, try wearing this stone on a necklace so that it is with you at all times. On the days you need more motivation, place the stone in your dominant hand and repeat your mantra.

3. **Citrine**
   A final way to use crystals for motivation is to combine citrine with essential oils. When these are combined, it can help you improve your motivation and your focus. While each person is different, you can try a lemon or orange oil to get you started. You will want to diffuse the oil as you meditate. Once in place, hold the citrine near your solar plexus and repeat your mantra until you feel motivated.

Negativity

Negativity can come into our lives in a number of forms. Sometimes, this energy comes from other people while other times, it comes from events that happen to us. One thing for sure is that these negative energies can drain us, making it almost impossible to focus on the things in life that really matter. On top of that, you probably don't feel well if you are living in a negative space. There are crystals that can help transform your negative energy into positive energy.

Mantra:

I choose to be a positive person. Everything I say and do, I will do in a positive manner.

Healing Stones:

1. **Smoky Quartz**
   Smoky quartz is one of the most popular stones to use for negative energy. It is a stone you can have all around your house to help create a positive space to work in. I suggest placing it under your bed or even under your desk at work!

2. **Hematite**
   Hematite stones have the ability to absorb negative energy. It can work on your own negative energy, negative energy from your environment, or even another individual. There are special hematite rings you can purchase if you tend to be in a negative space more than you would like — all you need to do is place the ring on your finger and state your mantra.

3. **Himalayan Salt**
   Another way to rid of negative energy in a space is to purchase a Himalayan salt lamp. You will want to place this lamp in the rooms that you spend the most time in. When the lightbulb heats up the Himalayan salt, it sends a positive energy field through the room, helping cleanse any negative energy and creates a positive space.

Patience

We have all lost our patience at some point in our lives. Whether it was with a co-worker, a child, or a loved one, it happens! Under certain circumstances, anyone can lack patience. If you find your patience is being tried, some crystals can help when you need a little extra support.

Mantra:

Everything is temporary. This feeling will pass.

Healing Stones:

1. **Howlite**

   Howlite is a stone that has the ability to teach anyone patience. If you have a lifestyle that is filled with impatience, this is the perfect stone for you. Whether you are dealing with crazy parking lots, yelling children, or a stressful situation at work, howlite can give you the support you need. All you will need to do is keep a smooth piece of howlite on your person. As the impatience starts to build, treat the stone as a worry stone and rub your thumb over it. When you rub the stone, repeat your mantra and become mindful of the patience you need for any given situation.

2. **Amazonite**

   Some people lack patience, in general. If you find that you are typically an impatient person, amazonite may be the crystal to benefit you most. This stone has the ability to sooth the highest of nerves. The energy of this stone helps with patience and grants the ability to help you chill out. You can keep the stone in your pocket or sleep with it under your bed to experience the most benefit.

3. **Labradorite**

   There will be times in your life when you need to be kind and patience with yourself. Labradorite can be helpful with this and can act as a reminder to be patient. Many people wear labradorite as jewelry so that they always have it on their person. If you find that you need patience with yourself, try holding the stone in your non-dominant hand and tell yourself, I am at peace. I am going to be patient.

Regret

In life, we have emotions that simply don't help us at all. Regret is one of these emotions. Unfortunately, this emotion stems from unresolved shame or guilt that sticks with us. When we fail to focus on life and instead, dwell of something we have already done, it can keep you from living your best life. When you regret, you are keeping yourself rooted in the past as opposed to the here and now, where you should be. Self-forgiveness is very important, and some crystals can help with this problem.

Mantra:

I choose to forgive myself. I will live in the here and now. I will let go of my past.

Healing Stones:

1. Rose Quartz

One major aspect of letting go of regret is having self-compassion. When you have self-compassion, you will be able to release regret sooner. As you already learned, rose quartz is a popular stone that will help you forgive yourself and release any regret you are holding onto. For this to work, you must place the rose quartz on your heart, close your eyes, and repeat your mantra.

2. Smoky Quartz

Another benefit of smoky quartz is the stone's ability to help you release any old beliefs you may be holding onto. For many, regret is an old belief that is no longer serving you in the here and the now. If you feel regret over something that happened in your past, try carrying a piece of smoky quartz in your pocket for quick access. If you ever feel regret slipping into your mind, hold the stone in your dominant hand and repeat your mantra until this emotion fades.

Healing Grid:

If you still feel regret and feel you need something a bit stronger to help you overcome these emotions, a releasing regret grid may do the trick for you. I suggest creating this grid under your bed or on a flat surface you spend a lot of time near.

Configuration: Triangle, to connect your spirit, mind, and body.

Stones Needed:

- Smoky Quartz (Focus Stone)
- Aquamarine (Intention Stone)
- Black Tourmaline (Perimeter Stones)

Rejection

When we get rejected, it can hurt a lot. Sometimes, we are rejected in relationships. Other times, we are rejected by things like a job. It can be very hard to put yourself out there when you risk rejection. It is important to realize that rejection is just a part of life. More than likely, you are rejected because you are meant for something different, something better! Nonetheless, rejection is still painful. If you fear rejection, it can hold you back from trying new things. Below, we will go over some crystals that can help you overcome your fear of rejection, so you can get out there and experience life to the fullest.

Mantra:

I am not afraid of rejection. I can take risks that benefit me. I am brave.

Healing Stones:

1. **Rose Quartz**

   When we are rejected by someone or something, we typically take that emotion to heart. Unfortunately, we have no control over whether people like us or not, but that doesn't mean that we don't get hurt when this happens. Rose quartz is the perfect stone to use to help heal the pain you feel. After rejection, it will be important to return to an emotion of self-love. If you feel the sting of rejection, try to wear rose quartz as jewelry. As the emotion creeps in, hold onto the stone and remind yourself that you are loved, and this rejection is not a reflection of yourself.

2. **Hematite**

   We have all experienced rejection at some point in our lives. Some develop a deep fear of rejection and avoid any risky situations to avoid this feeling. Fear is rooted deep in our root chakra and is associated with our need for safety and security. The hematite stone is able to provide us with both. To use this stone, place it in your non-dominant hand and repeat your mantra. As you do this, you will want to visualize this fear of rejection like a cloud over your head. Imagine that this cloud flows from above you and into the stone, releasing all of your fear. Once you release your fear of rejection, you can do more exciting things in life.

3. Yellow Tigers Eye

Along with the heart, rejection can also affect our self-worth and self-imagine. These emotions are typically located in our solar plexus. You can use a yellow tiger's eye stone to help strengthen this chakra. By doing this, you can overcome past rejections and the pain that it has caused you. The more you practice getting over the fear of rejection, the less likely this fear will cripple you in the future. You can practice by placing the crystal over your solar plexus chakra. As you lay down, imagine the energy from the stone flowing into your body and strengthening your self-worth. When you do this, you will want to tell yourself that there is no amount of rejection that can keep you down.

Stress

In general, life can be pretty stressful at times. If you think about it, we stress about a lot of small things throughout the day. We stress about getting to work on time, we stress about getting the kids ready for school, we even stress about what we are going to eat! When life seems to be spiraling out of control and you feel yourself falling apart, there is a crystal that can help you in this situation. When you manage stress properly, you can increase your health.

Mantra:

I choose to let this stress go. I will be healthy and happy.

Healing Stones:

1. Yellow Tiger's Eye

When you are stressed, this has a major effect on your adrenal gland. The part of your chakra that is associated with your adrenal glands is your solar plexus. The stone of yellow tiger's eye has the ability to absorb any excess energy you may be taking in. When there is too much energy, it causes stress from an imbalance of energy. The stone is able to absorb this energy and helps you rebalance in the process. For this stone to work, simply lay down where you are most comfortable and place the stone over your solar plexus chakra. As you relax, take a deep breath and repeat your mantra to yourself until you begin to feel balanced.

2. Smoky Quartz

As you have already learned up to this point, smoky quartz has many amazing qualities. Another benefit of this stone is that it has the ability to stabilize energy. When the world feels like it is spinning around you, the stone can help you regain your balance. For some people, they enter the fight-or-flight mode when they are stressed out. The stone will help prevent this from happening in the first place when used properly. Many people choose to wear this stone to feel balanced throughout the day. If you ever find yourself in a situation you can't handle, take the stone in your hand, close your eyes, and state your mantra. You can do this for as long as you need until you feel a sense of calm wash over you.

3. Hematite

Another response to stress is fear. Luckily, the stone Hematite has the ability to absorb this fear if it is something you ever experience. For this to work, simply place the stone in your non-dominant hand and squeeze it. When you close your eyes, imagine that there is a black cloud over you. Once you see the cloud, imagine the cloud flowing through you and into your stone. You will want to meditate until this emotion vanishes, and you are feeling peaceful and stress-free again.

Trust

Trust is a hard concept for a lot of people. Unfortunately, there are some events we can go through that create a lack of trust in our future. Some traumas affect us emotionally, mentally, and sometimes, physically. When this happens, it can be hard to trust other people or even feel safe around them. Some crystals can help you build your trust in people. By working on the issue, you may find yourself feeling safe and secure in more situations.

Mantra:

I am safe. I am loved. I place my trust in the universe.

Healing Stones:

1. **Garnet**

   It is believed that our sense of security and safety comes from our root chakra. When we lack trust, it may mean that our root chakra is out of whack. In order to restore trust in humanity, you will need to restore the energy in your root chakra to feel safe. Garnet is the perfect stone to accomplish this task. For this crystal to work, you will want to begin your meditation on your back and place the stone near your root chakra. When you feel safe and secure in your location, you can close your eyes and state your mantra. You will want to repeat this mantra until you feel better.

2. **Carnelian**

   While sometimes our trust issues are with other people, these trust issues can also stem from our selves. Sometimes, we break promises we keep for ourselves, and often lack trust in our own integrity. This lack of trust with yourself comes from your sacral chakra. Carnelian is one stone that may be able to help with this lack of trust in yourself. For this stone to work, you can use it while you are meditating. All you will need to do is lie down on your back, place the stone near your sacral chakra, and repeat your mantra. You can change the above mantra to become more fitting for your own being. You can try something like, I trust myself because I will always keep my word.

3. **Amethyst**

   If none of these situations match you, perhaps, you just lack the universe in general. If you are fearful to leave your house or trust anyone in your life, Amethyst is a stone that can help you connect to the universe. The universe is always there for you, even when it feels as though it is acting against you. For this stone to work, try placing it against your third eye chakra and take a few moments to meditate. Repeat your mantra until you feel a sense of trust flow through you. Even if you can't trust others, always place your trust in the universe.

You have noticed through this chapter that a lot of our issues seem to stem from a lack of balance in our chakra. If you have no idea what your chakras are or what they do, you are not alone! In the next chapter, I will be teaching you everything you need to know. We will go over each chakra, what they do for you, and how to balance them out. Once you learn about your chakras, you will get a sense of the crystals you need, and then we can get started on learning the crystals and their incredible benefits as well!

CHAPTER THREE

Chakra Connections And Crystals

In the prior chapter, you may have been shaking your head, wondering what all this talk about our chakras was. Believe it or not, chakras actually have a huge impact on your daily life. When energy is blocked in any of your chakras, this can have major effects on you spiritually, mentally, emotionally, and even physically. In order to balance your chakras, you will need to have a further understanding of them and how they work.

The first lesson you will need to learn is that we are more than just our physical body.

Our chakras, much like everything else in the universe, are created through energy. Everything from our atoms to our organs, to our muscles, is all made up of energy. Your whole entire body is an energy field that can expand past your physical body. While the physical is made in intricate layers such as the skeletal system, the nervous system, and musculature, the energy within your body is a whole other complicated layer. Together, all of these layers of energy are called your aura. While this aura does interact with your physical body, it is also a part of your chakras.

In Sanskrit, the word chakra means wheel. These energy centers within your body are known as energy vortexes. The vortexes have the ability to transport energy from your body and aura into the universe. If it helps, picture your chakra system like a bloodstream of your spirit. The system helps you balance and regulate your body.

While all living things have a chakra system, we will be focusing on yours today. Within your body, you have seven major chakras. There are also other minor ones, but we won't throw too much at you for now. Each major chakra in your system is connected to certain glands and organs. This holds true for the physical dysfunctions of these systems whether they are spiritual, mental, or even emotional.

As you learn more about your chakras, you will be able to tell where your imbalances may be stemming from. By using crystals, you will be mindful of your healing through not only your mind but your spirit too. While physical activities can help some of your issues, cleaning your spirit via crystals may work wonders for you too. For now, we will start with the basics of the chakras.

Feeling the Energy

Before we rocket off into learning all about the chakras, it is time to learn your own energy. As you first start, try to get in touch with the energy within your body. You can do this by holding your hands together and have your palms face one another. As you do this, you may notice slight warmth exchanging between your hands. If you don't, don't worry! It will take some time and practice. Once you do feel the heat between your hands, separate your hands a little more and stretch the energy between your palms. When you feel comfortable with this motion, you can then try to condense the energy by bringing your palms closer together. Feel free to repeat this a few times until you feel comfortable with your energy.

Before Getting Started

As a beginner, you may feel nervous about engaging with your chakras. There are a few factors to remember as you get started. The first detail to remember is that you must be patient with yourself. There are many people who try to learn too much at once! It will be important to understand that you should never judge yourself when it seems as though you are "failing." You are on your own timeline. Everything is happening exactly as it should; this includes your healing with crystals.

No matter how hard you try, healing simply isn't something that you can speed up. Instead, try to focus on the healing journey. As you practice and take more steps toward healing, you may learn more about yourself than you ever thought was possible. Your transformation is going to take both compassion and patience, remember to always be kind to yourself.

With that being said, it will also be vital that you never push yourself out of your comfort zone. There are repercussions to forcing your energy, and you will most likely burn yourself out. Of course, you are probably very eager to connect to your chakras, but you will want to take your time. Much like learning the energy between your hands, you will be learning how to connect to each chakra. If you push too hard, you could potentially give yourself a headache. If you find practicing is too stressful and you feel resistance to the energy, try taking a break and then come back to the practice.

Finally, it is important to point out that at some points, you may need a professional. While there is a lot you can accomplish on your own, guidance is always helpful. This is especially true if you ever hit a point where you feel like you are hitting a wall. If you do choose to go down this path, you will want to be sure that the practitioner is certified or licensed. Luckily with the internet, you can check out their reviews before you make an appointment. Once you meet them, remember that certain people will be a better fit for you than others. You should always take your time and choose what is best for you, not what other people say is best for you. With those bits of advice, it is time to learn how to take matters into your own hands!

Activating Kundalini Energy

As stated earlier, the foundation of your chakra system is made up of seven different chakras. Each one of these chakras serves a purpose, but they are also all interconnected as you will be learning later in this chapter. Before we get into each chakra, you will need to learn how to activate your kundalini energy.

What is kundalini energy, you may be asking? It is the energy that has the ability to awaken your chakras. While all of us have this energy within us, it is often dormant and coiled at the base of our spine. As you work with your chakras, you will begin to awaken this energy.

It should be noted that this energy doesn't just suddenly awaken one day. This process will take a period of time and will require constant practice through your life. You can do this by performing energy work on yourself or going to a yoga class every week.

For other people, kundalini energy can be awakened randomly. If you are not prepared for this to happen, it could block your chakras or become stuck in a certain area. When this happens, it can cause some painful symptoms caused by the surge of energy. It can also cause mental and physical instability. This is why it is vital to start slow and work overtime with your practice. Once you begin, you will learn how to send this energy in beneficial ways. For now, we will get started with one of your basic chakras; the root chakra.

Root Chakra

The root chakra is one of the first physical chakras you have. This chakra is in charge of your sense of safety and security. When this chakra is out of harmony, you may feel that you cannot trust the universe around you. At points, you may feel ungrounded and have issues in creating relationships with people around you. It also creates a false sense of understanding your basic needs like shelter, love, and food. You will begin to function out of fear as opposed to love.

When this chakra is balanced, you will start to feel grounded again. You will be able to move with the ebb and flow of life and trust the people around you again. A balanced root chakra also helps you connect with family and loved ones when you feel safe again.

1. **Location**
   Your root chakra is located at the base of your spine.

2. **Color**
   Red

3. **Element**
   Earth

4. **Other Names**
   You may notice through research that the root chakra has several names it can be referred to as. Some other names include the first chakra, base chakra, and Muladhara, which is the Sanskrit name for root chakra.

5. **Physical Body Parts**
   Your root chakra is in charge of several body parts including the base of the spine, rectum, feet, bones, legs, your immune system, the large intestine, and your teeth.

6. **Physical Dysfunction**
   Unfortunately, an imbalance of the root chakra can show in several different physical dysfunctions. These include

weight problems, depression, immune disorders, knee issues, arthritis, constipation, rectal tumors, varicose veins, back pain, and more.

7. **Emotional and Mental Dysfunctions**
   On top of the physical dysfunctions that come from an imbalance in your root chakra, it can also block the ability for you to stand up for yourself, to provide life's necessities, or experience safety and security. These may stem from an energy block from fear or guilt.

8. **Crystals**
   Some of the following crystals can help bring balance back into your life if you feel your root chakra is blocked or out of whack.
   Fire Agate, Smoky Quartz, Lodestone, Red Jasper, Onyx, Obsidian, Hematite, Bloodstone, Black Tourmaline, Garnet, Ruby.

Sacral Plexus Chakra

Your solar plexus chakra is located just above the root chakra. This chakra is in charge of your reproductive and sexual activities. The chakra can also play a major role in your creativity and your emotions. You may feel your sacral plexus chakra is out of balance if you feel the inability to express your feelings. At some points in your life, you may feel you are holding onto anger and are out of touch of the things that have brought you pleasure in life. If you feel stifled in your creativity or are experiencing relationship issues, this could be the root of the problem.

Once you have balanced this chakra, you will have the ability to get in touch with the pleasurable things in life again. When you return to a balanced state, you will be able to grow healthy relationships and connect to others socially and sexually. It will also help you develop a healthy relationship with life and money.

1. **Location**
   Your sacral plexus chakra is located about two inches under your navel.

48

2. Color
Orange

3. Element
Water

4. Other Names
The sacral plexus chakra has been known to be referred to by several other names. These names include naval chakra, pelvic chakra, sacral chakra, second chakra, or Svadisthana.

5. Physical Body Parts
Kidneys, hips, bladder, appendix, pelvis, lower vertebra, womb, and genitals.

6. Physical Dysfunction
An imbalance of the sacral plexus chakra can lead to a few physical dysfunctions. These can include kidney issues, bladder issues, impotence, pelvic pain, gynecological issues, and even lower back pain.

7. Emotional and Mental Dysfunction
On top of the physical ailments, you may find that an imbalance of this chakra can have effects on your emotional and mental states as well. Some of these issues include ethics, relationship honor, creativity, lack of power and control, issues with sex, money problems, guilt emotions, and even blame of other people. It is thought that these blocks of energy can stem from issues like rape, trauma, sexual abuse, or gender issues.

8. Crystals
Luckily, several crystals can help you if you feel that this chakra is out of balance. Some of these crystals include Sunstone, orange tourmaline, coral, moonstone, amber, and carnelian.

Solar Plexus Chakra

The next chakra we will be going over is the solar plexus chakra. This chakra is in charge of your sense of worth, self-esteem, and your personality. When this chakra is out of harmony, an individual may feel the need to have constant control and will dominate any situation. If you feel the need to keep up with your appearance and be better than others, your chakra may be out of balance! A block of this chakra often creates an overwhelming feeling of being inadequate, and with this emotion, you may not respect yourself. The opposite can be true for others, as an imbalance of the solar plexus chakra could cause you to give your powers to others if you feel no sense of self.

Once your solar plexus chakra is back in harmony, you may feel a sense of wholeness again. You will learn how to cultivate your power in a healthy way and gain a sense of self-worth. When this chakra is balanced, there is a healthy balance between the material world and the spiritual world. At this point, you will feel true calmness and inner peace within your soul.

1. **Location**
   Your solar plexus chakra is located two inches above your navel.

2. **Color**
   Yellow

3. **Element**
   Fire

4. **Other Names**
   The solar plexus chakra can be referred to as the power chakra, the third chakra, or its Sanskrit name, Manipura.

5. **Physical Body Part**
   Middle spine, spleen, gallbladder, liver, upper intestines, stomach, and the abdomen.

6. **Physical Dysfunction**
   If your solar plexus chakra is out of balance, you may be experiencing some of the several health issues: diabetes, hepatitis, fatigue, adrenal dysfunction, liver dysfunction,

bulimia, anorexia, indigestion, intestinal problems, colon issues, gastric ulcers, or arthritis.

7. **Emotional and Mental Dysfunction**
On top of the ailments mentioned above, you could also be experiencing some of the emotional dysfunctions listed such as lack of personal honor, sensitivity to criticism, a lack of responsibility to make decisions, lack of self-care, lack of self-respect, no self-confidence, lowered self-esteem, a sense of intimidation from others and a lack of trust and/or fear. It is believed that these issues can occur due to issues of control, repressed anger, or issues of control related to power.

8. **Crystals**
If you experience any of the above physical, mental, or emotional dysfunctions, some crystals can help you out. These crystals include Rutilated Quartz, Yellow Agate, Yellow Tiger's Eye, Yellow Topaz, Amber, and Yellow Citrine.

The Heart Chakra

Next, we will be going over the heart chakra. You may already be aware, but this chakra is in charge of the physical and spiritual aspects of our beings. The heart chakra is a pivotal location as it connects both your spiritual and physical chakra. If you are looking to get in touch with your Higher Self, the heart chakra is where you will want to look.

When the heart chakra is out of harmony with the rest of the chakras, you may be feeling like you are disconnected from yourself. An imbalance of this chakra may make you feel like you are not deserving of love and cannot love yourself properly. Many people who experience this, become depressed and lose touch of who they truly are.

Once your heart chakra is back in harmony, you will be able to cultivate joy in your life. With the balance, you will be able to love and accept yourself for who you really are. It is only at this point that you will be able to not only give but also receive the love that

51

you deserve. Once you are in balance, you will understand what it means to have compassion for yourself and others in the universe.

1. **Location**
   It is located in the center of your chest.

2. **Color**
   Green

3. **Element**
   Air

4. **Other Names**
   It can be referred to by its Sanskrit name, Anahata or the fourth chakra.

5. **Physical Body Parts**
   The Heart chakra is in charge of your diaphragm, breasts, ribs, shoulders, arms, lungs, the circulatory system, and of course, the heart.

6. **Physical Dysfunction**
   If your heart chakra is out of balance, it is possible that you could be having the following physical dysfunctions. These include high blood pressure, breast cancer, lung disease, pneumonia, lung cancer, asthma, allergies, heart disease, heart attack, or heart failure.

7. **Emotional or Mental Dysfunction**
   Some of the emotional or mental dysfunctions you can experience due to the heart chakra being out of harmony could include lack of trust, no hope, zero compassion toward others, a sense of loneliness, being self-centered, grief, resentment, and hatred for everyone. It is thought that the potential cause of energy block in this location could be due to heartache or even grief.

8. **Crystals**
   If you suffer from any of the ailments above, some crystals can help you in this situation. The crystals include Peridot,

Green Kyanite, Green Calcite, Jade, Green Tourmaline, Emerald, or Rose Quartz.

The Throat Chakra

Now, it is time to move into learning the first spiritual chakra. The throat chakra is in charge of our authentic voice, our faith, and our understanding of others. When this chakra is out of harmony, it may become difficult to speak the truth and to express yourself. If you have recently been feeling that you are out of touch with your will to live, this chakra may be imbalanced.

Once you balance the chakra, you will be able to speak your truth and follow your dreams. When your values are in place, you have the strength to say what you mean and express yourself to others in an authentic manner. You must learn the delicate balance between speech and silence and when it is appropriate for each action.

1. **Location**
   The throat chakra is located in the hollow of your collarbone and at the front of the base of your neck.

2. **Color**
   Light Blue

3. **Element**
   Sound

4. **Other Names**
   The throat chakra is referred to as Vishuddha in Sanskrit and also the fifth chakra.

5. **Physical Body Part**
   The throat chakra is in charge of the hands, arms, shoulders, esophagus, hypothalamus, teeth, gums, mouth, neck vertebrae, the trachea, and the throat.

6. **Physical Dysfunction**
   If your throat chakra is out of balance, you may experience thyroid problems or swollen glands. It is also possible you

could develop a stiff neck, TMJ, scoliosis, gym difficulties, mouth ulcers, a sore throat, or a raspy voice.

7. **Emotional and Mental Dysfunction**
   If you don't have any of the physical dysfunctions from above, there are also some dysfunctions that can happen mentally or emotionally. These issues include lack of faith, criticism, judgment, addiction, inability to make a decision, problems with following your dreams or losing your will. It is thought that these blocks can come from suppressing your creative talent, swallowing your words, or never expressing yourself.

8. **Crystals**
   If you suffer from any of the dysfunctions from above, there are several crystals that may be able to help you out. Some of the crystals include Lapis Lazuli, Sodalite, Iolite, Celestite, Aquamarine, Blue Kyanite, and even Turquoise.

The Third Eye Chakra

As we move up your chakras, the next one is the third eye chakra. Often times, this chakra is associated with your sixth sense which is in charge of your intuition, spiritual insight, as well as your wisdom. You may notice that this chakra is unbalanced if you find yourself lacking faith in your own intuition. Often times, people who have energy blocked to their sixth chakra only have the ability to see their physical reality. When this happens, it is possible you may fear your own inner wisdom.

With the help of crystals, you may be able to return your awareness and intuition. It is vital that you trust your inner vision and allow your intuition to guide you through life. As we mentioned before, there is so much more than what we can just physically see.

1. **Location**
   The third eye chakra is located between your eyebrows.

2. **Color**
   Indigo

3. **Element**

Light

4. Other Names
The third chakra is often referred to as the sixth chakra, forehead chakra, or brow chakra. It can also be called by the Sanskrit name, Ajna.

5. Physical Body Parts
This chakra is in charge of your nose, ears, eyes, brain, and the whole nervous system.

6. Physical Dysfunction
If your third eye chakra is blocked or imbalanced, you could be experiencing some of the following physical dysfunctions. These include blurred vision, headaches, seizures, learning disabilities, spinal difficulties, deafness, blindness, neurological issues, stroke, or even brain tumors.

7. Emotional and Mental Dysfunction
An imbalanced third eye chakra could also lead to some mental and emotional disturbances. It's possible you lack the ability to learn from new experiences, have the inability to open to others, have some feelings of inadequacy, doubt your intellectual abilities, lack the ability to evaluate yourself or feel you can never tell the truth. It is believed that these issues are caused by a lack of intuition.

8. Crystals
Kyanite, Star Sapphire, Clear Quartz, Tanzanite, Sugilite, Lepidolite, Fluorite, Amethyst, Lapis Lazuli

The Crown Chakra

As mentioned earlier, there are several other chakras, but the crown chakra is the last of the major chakras. This chakra is the source which connects to your higher self and the Divine. When this chakra is out of harmony, you may feel the sense that you are disconnected from your self as well as the universe. Perhaps, lately, you have been feeling angry at God. You feel lost and feel life has become difficult. If you feel depressed and alone, your crown chakra may be creating all of these feelings.

Once you balance your crown chakra, you will begin to connect to the universe again. It is important to understand that you are an individual and you will need to trust the path you are on. Our identity is so much more than just our physical form. When you are able to love and accept yourself for who you are, it will be easier to elevate your consciousness.

1. **Location**
   This chakra is located at the top of your head, in the center.

2. **Color**
   Gold, white, and purple.

3. **Element**
   Thought

4. **Other Names**
   Seventh Chakra or Sahasrara

5. **Physical Body Parts**
   The crown chakra is in charge of your central nervous system, the cerebral cortex, skeletal system, and the muscular system.

6. **Physical Dysfunction**
   If your crown chakra is out of balance, you may experience several physical dysfunctions. These issues range from the sense of alienation, apathy, confusion, sensitivity to your environment, physical disorder, chronic exhaustion, depression, and other energetic disorders.

7. **Emotional and Mental Dysfunctions**
   With these physical dysfunctions, it is also possible you may be experiencing emotional dysfunctions from a blocked chakra. You could lack devotion, spirituality, faith, or seeing the bigger picture. You may also have the inability to trust your ethics or values, lack courage, and

act selfishly. These issues seem to stem from a lack of trust in the Divine or an unresolved anger.

8. Crystals
White Topaz, Apophyllite, Kunzite, Phenacite, Selenite, Moonstone, Labradorite, Herkimer Diamond, Clear Quartz, Amethyst.

Using Crystals to Heal Chakras

As you can tell, there is a certain magic when you combine crystals with your internal energy. This is because crystals have the ability to draw out energy and can also redirect it when needed. When this happens, you will be able to develop the strength with the associated stone. On top of these wonderful benefits, the crystals can also help you heal these issues and rebalance your energy.

The whole reason for working with crystals is to help you engage with the Earth, and its natural energy. When you practice this, you will be able to nourish any of your natural gifts and strengths. As you practice more, remember that it will be important to release emotions that no longer serve you. Once your energy is restored and rebalanced, you will be able to tap into your gifts and elevate your consciousness.

Luckily, there are a few different ways to work with crystals, as mentioned slightly in the previous chapter. You may have noted that one of the most popular ways to use a crystal is to keep it on your person. When shopping, you will notice all the different types of jewelry like bracelets, earrings, or pendants. If you aren't a jewelry person, you can always carry the crystal in your pocket.

Another major way to use crystals to heal your chakras is through meditation. When you combine crystals with meditation, the crystal will amplify the energy you are working on, whether you are looking to gain energy or release it. Remember that practice will help you out in the long run. You won't be a master after a couple of sessions and that is okay!

The pros of using crystals to heal your chakras are that they are incredibly versatile to work with. On top of that, they are also aesthetically pleasing. Many people enjoy crystals to heal themselves because they are easy to use, and the healing power can be easily felt. As you begin, you may also feel the pulsing in your hand that holds the crystals.

The downfall of using crystals is that it will take some time to become familiar with crystals. Remember that as you start your collection, it will take some time before you find the right crystals that work for you. The crystals you buy will vary depending on the individual. I suggest you do your research before you dive into any big purchases. This is exactly why in the next chapter, we will be going over a number of crystals. With all of the information within these pages, you will be able to buy the crystals that work best for you!

CHAPTER FOUR

Crystals To Know

In this chapter, we will be listing off different crystals in alphabetical order. As you will see, each crystal will have their own color, physical cures, mental cures, and affirmations. In the chapter above, we went over several of the different ailments crystals can be used for. It will be up to you to take this information and apply it to your life. I hope that within this chapter, you will be able to find at least one crystal to help you.

Actinolite

This crystal is best known for its shielding properties. Actinolite has the ability to fill gaps of energy that may be in your chakras, resulting in unwanted negativity, illness, and stress. The crystal can help you balance your spirit, body, and mind. It also can boost self-esteem by releasing negative energy you may be holding onto.

1. **Chakra**
   Heart Chakra

2. **Color**
   Black and Green

3. **Rarity**
   Common

4. **Physical Uses**
   Actinolite is excellent for several physical ailments. Some of the more common usages are to strengthen the immune system. It can also help if you have kidney problems, liver problems, or cancer.

5. **Emotional Uses**
   This crystal has been known to help refuse stress and tension. It is also great to help individuals cope with change and find harmony in their life. On top of these wonderful benefits, actinolite is also excellent if you lack self-confidence or self-worth.

6. Spiritual Uses
Actinolite is wonderful to help with the following spiritual issues you may be experiencing. These ailments include lack of visualization, shielding, growth, balance, or awareness. The crystal can also help remove any energy blocks you may be experiencing.

Agate

Agate is a crystal that is most commonly known for its quiet energy. If you are looking to achieve balance and stability in your life, agate will be the perfect crystal for you. Many individuals use this stone as it works on the cause of an issue as opposed to the symptom of the problem. This crystal can work on mental functions and improve clarity. It should be noted that while the energy of this crystal works slowly due to the gentle nature, it works very deliberately and will have a lasting impact when used correctly.

1. Chakra
Agate comes in several colors and will work with different chakras depending on the color.

2. Color
Yellow, White, Light Brown, Red, Pink, Orange, Green, Brown, Blue, Black

3. Rarity
Common

4. Physical Uses
This crystal is excellent for a number of physical ailments. These issues include problems with the uterus, constipation, diarrhea, stomach issues, skin infections, rheumatism, pancreas problems, gastritis, eye infections, digestion health, blood vessels, and aids.

5. Emotional Uses
With these physical fixes, agate can also help with some emotional ailments. It can help you tell the truth, helps work through trauma, has the ability to soothe stressed out individuals, can increase self-confident, enhance

perception, increase courage, helps with bitterness, and grants the ability to release any anger you may be holding onto.

6. **Emotional Uses**
   Agate can help bring balance and clarity back into your life. It also helps ground individuals and helps them grow to become their true selves.

Amazonite

This crystal is best used if you struggle with non-verbal expression. Often times, amazonite is used to connect to Nature Spirits and is known as the stone of success and abundance. It has the ability to attract good luck and focus, leading to a peaceful transition, especially if your time on earth is coming to an end. This crystal can assist in balancing your yin and yang energies and restore any separation you may have from the Divine.

1. **Chakra**
   Heart Chakra and Throat Chakra

2. **Color**
   Turquoise and Green

3. **Rarity**
   Common

4. **Physical Uses**
   Amazonite can help with a wide range of physical ailments. On top of helping with the yin and yang energy, it can also help to balance the thyroid health, reflexology, osteoporosis, nutrient absorption, nervous system regeneration, muscle pains, mental clarity, liver disorders, heart issues, gout, dental problems, breast health, balance issues, and even can assist with chemotherapy.

5. **Emotional Uses**
   If you are looking to use amazonite with emotional uses, it is also incredibly versatile here. Amazonite can help with worrying, trauma, helps soothe stress, can boost self-confidence, increase joy, decrease fear, helps cope with

grief, can help guild compassion, build communication, creates clarity, and can help you release anger you may be holding onto.

6. **Spiritual Uses**
   With these wonderful benefits, amazonite can also help with balance, clarity, universal love, manifestation, and grants an enhanced intuition.

Amber

Amber is one of the more popular healing crystals. It is an excellent crystal to add to your collection if you are a beginner, as it has gentle energy and can help heal and cleanse. Amber is also versatile as it has the ability to aid in physical healing as well as emotional healing and environmental clearing. On top of these wonderful benefits, amber is also very protective and can help promote fertility.

1. **Chakra**
   Solar Plexus Chakra

2. **Color**
   Orange and Yellow

3. **Rarity**
   Common

4. **Physical Uses**
   Amber can help with a number of physical ailments. As mentioned earlier, this crystal is very versatile. It can help with viruses, urinary tract health, trauma, toxins, tonsillitis, throat issues, stomach issues, spleen problems, skin infections, pregnancy, pneumonia, pancreas health, pain relief, ovarian disorders, nervous system problems, lungs, laryngitis, intestinal disorders, infections, immune system strengthening, headaches, migraines, gallbladder issues, ear infections, dental pains, colds, breathing problems, brain disorders, bone disorders, birthing issues, asthma, arthritis, and even wounds.

5. **Emotional Uses**

Amber is an excellent crystal to use if you are looking to reduce tension or stress in your life. It can also help individuals with their patience and can help ease depression. If you need to increase patience or help with grounding, amber is a great crystal to add to your collection.

6. Spiritual Uses
This crystal is used often for people to help balance their aura. It is also thought to help with ancient wisdom and knowledge if that is something you're seeking. Amber is also used to help recall past life events, which helps some people heal in their own ways.

Amethyst

Amethyst is the first crystal many metaphysicians choose to use due to its protective and powerful nature. Often times, amethyst was used in ancient times to help people with addictions and is now known as the stone of sobriety. This crystal has strong healing energy that can help transform any negative energy in your spirit into love energy. If you feel that your third eye chakra is out of balance, amethyst has the ability to provide the peaceful energy you will need for meditation. It can also be used to activate the crown chakra to connect to the Divine and enhance your spiritual awareness.

1. Chakra
Third Eye Chakra and Crown Chakra

2. Color
Purple and Lavender

3. Rarity
Common

4. Physical Uses
Amethyst is excellent for a number of physical uses. It can help with some of the following issues such as wrinkle, overall well-being, weakness, viruses, tumors, swelling, smoking addiction, sleep issues, skin infections, respiratory health, post-surgery healing, pituitary gland problems, pain relief, issues with overindulgence, night terrors, mental

health, itching, insomnia, injuries, supports the immune system, hormone production, hearing issues, headaches, endocrine system problems, eczema, digestion, the dying process, cancer, burns, bruising, brain disorders, alcoholism, addiction, and acne!

5. **Emotional Uses**
With these physical benefits, amethyst is also a powerful crystal to help with emotional ailments you may be experiencing. Some of the more popular issues that amethyst benefits include increasing inner serenity, reducing stress, defusing rage, increases peace, helps with focus, increases love, motivation, and decreases night terrors. It can also be used to help release negativity, creates emotional balance, helps cope with loss, copes with grief, and increases your ability to cope with change or anxiety you may be experiencing.

6. **Spiritual Uses**
Amethyst is a popular stone to help with spiritual ailments. It can help increase wisdom, telekinesis, increases spiritual protection, and is used very often in meditation. This crystal also helps enhance psychic abilities, increases intuition, and can bring individuals cosmic awareness if that is something they are searching for. Amethyst also helps people open up to their own awareness and can help you connect to your inner child. It is also used for astral projection and can help individuals interpret and recall their dreams.

Aquamarine

When you find aquamarine crystals, you may notice that they resonate with the ocean. The energy of this crystal connects to the spirit of the sea. Historically, seamen carried this crystal to help travel safe in the water and were meant to protect them from drowning. This crystal is known as the stone of courage and protection. Most times, it helps promote self-expression and can enhance communication blocks you may be experiencing. It is also a very popular crystal to help enhance and align your chakras.

1. **Chakras**
Throat Chakra and Heart Chakra

2. Color
Turquoise and Blue

3. Rarity
Common

4. Physical Uses
Aquamarine is used for a number of physical ailments. Some of these issues it can benefit include water retention, traveling, thyroid issues, skin infections, sinus problems, issues with the pituitary gland, neck issues, nausea, liver disorders, jaw problems, foot problems, eye disorders, edema, eczema, dental problems, brain disorders, issues with the bladder, allergies, acne, and other autoimmune disorders.

5. Emotional Uses
While aquamarine does help with a number of physical problems, it is also great for emotional problems you may be experiencing. This crystal grants serenity, peace, inspiration, harmony, and can help individuals cope with changes. It is also excellent if you are looking to release anger you are holding onto or can help with any anxiety you may have.

6. Spiritual Uses
Aquamarine is a popular crystal people use to help communicate with angels. It can also help communicate with your higher-self, your inner child, or even just to use during meditation. As mentioned earlier, aquamarine is a great protector and helps give people the strength to tell the truth.

Black Tourmaline

You may have noticed that black tourmaline has been mentioned several times in this book already. This stone is an excellent source of protection and can help block any negative energy that comes your way. It also has the ability to remove this negative energy if it already exists in your person and assists to purify your energy into a lighter vibration. On top of these benefits, it is also used to help balance and harmonize your chakras.

1. **Chakra**
   Root Chakra

2. **Color**
   Black

3. **Rarity**
   Common

4. **Physical Uses**
   Black Tourmaline is mostly used for physical protection. It has also been known to help with physical ailments such as dyslexia, chemotherapy, arthritis, addiction, and radiation complications.

5. **Emotional Uses**
   As for emotional benefits, black tourmaline can help reduce any stress or tension you may be feeling. We also mentioned that this stone can help with anxiety, criticism, and can help balance your sense of serenity.

6. **Spiritual Uses**
   Black Tourmaline is mostly used for spiritual and psychic protection. It also has been known to help balance your aura and protect you from electromagnetic frequencies and pollution. There is also a belief that black tourmaline can protect you from aliens and other extraterrestrial communication!

Bloodstone

Bloodstone is an interesting crystal as it is composed of Chalcedony but also has small dots of Red Jasper. This stone has been used for thousands of years and is a powerful healing stone. Often times, it can be used if you are looking to detoxify and purify your body of any negative energy. It also has the ability to enhance clarity, brain function, and increases energy by removing any energy blocks you may have. As a beginner, this may be a good choice to start your crystal collection with.

1. Chakra
Heart Chakra, Solar Plexus Chakra, and the Sacral Chakra

2. Color
Red and Green

3. Rarity
Common

4. Physical Uses
Bloodstone has the ability to work on a wide variety of physical ailments. Some of the benefits include help with tumor growth, stroke, pancreas health, nose bleeds, muscle pain, lung issues, liver disorders, kidney disorders, immune strengthening, high blood pressure, heart issues, eye issues, colon issues, circulatory problems, cancer, bronchitis, body detox, blood disorders, blood clotting, blood cleansing, blood circulation, bleeding, and anemia.

5. Emotional and Spiritual Uses
With these wonderful physical benefits, bloodstone also comes with a few emotional benefits. Bloodstone can help increase compassion and courage. It also can help individuals become gentler by releasing any retained anger.

Bowenite

You may have heard of Bowenite before, as it is Rhode Island's state mineral. Often times, it can be confused with Jade, and while it is close in comparison, it is a variety of Antigorite. This crystal is a semi-precious stone and is usually made of a higher-grade material. Historically, this crystal was worn as an amulet as it has the ability to protect individuals from destructive forces. It also makes well for a dream stone and helps release emotions that may be suppressed.

1. Chakra
Heart Chakra

2. Color
Green

3. Rarity
Pretty Common

4. Physical Uses
Bowenite is the perfect crystal to use if you are looking to balance your masculinity or feminine attributes as it can help with your hormonal balance. It is also great to help regulate blood sugar and diabetes.

5. Emotional Uses
This crystal is wonderful if you are searching for protection from external forces. It can also help with relationships when it comes to love and friendships. Bowenite also has the ability to help with anxiety if that is something you have.

6. Spiritual Uses
One of the more common uses for bowenite is for spiritual protection. The crystal is also excellent for dream interpretation, as it has the ability to help enhance and recall dreams. It has also been known to help with shielding against negative forces.

Calcite

Calcite is most commonly known as an energy amplifier and cleanser. When this stone is used properly, it can help restore any negative energy whether it is in your house or your body. You can use this stone to remove any old patterns you may have to help increase personal drive and motivation. It is most commonly known as the Stone of the Mind. It can help increase your memory as well as learning abilities. If you are a student, this could be a useful stone to have in your collection.

1. Chakra
Varies depending on the color.

2. Color
Yellow, Sky Blue, Pink, Red, Peach, Orange, Green, Clear, Blue

3. Rarity
Common

4. Physical Uses
Calcite can help with several physical ailments. These include issues with the skeletal system, nutrient absorption, helps with mental clarity, joint pain, dental issues, and bone disorders.

5. Emotional and Spiritual Uses
This stone can help increase your motivation and ability to learn. It can also benefit you if you are looking to relax. Spiritual wise, Calcite is often used to help with long distance healing as its vibrations are fairly powerful.

Carnelian

Carnelian was a stone used back in ancient times to help the dead protect themselves as they traveled into the afterlife. It is believed that this stone has the ability to calm fears of death and rebirth. The powers of this stone grant the ability to accept the cycle of life and bring a sense of serenity about everything. Carnelian can also increase your physical energy as well as give you courage while boosting your creativity. Many people choose to wear this stone to enhance their vitality.

1. Chakra
Sacral Chakra

2. Color
Orange

3. Rarity
Common

4. Physical Uses
Many people choose to have carnelian in their crystal collection because it has so many incredible benefits. This stone can help with a number of physical ailments including weakness, urinary tract issues, tissue health, scoliosis, reproductive issues, pancreas health, ovarian disorders, memory problems, low blood pressure, liver disorders, kidney disorders, intestinal disorders, problems with infertility, infections, edema, colon disorders, colds, body

balance, blood circulation, back problems, appetite control, and even allergies.

5. **Emotional Uses**

Emotional wise, carnelian helps a lot with understanding death, as I mentioned before. It also helps many people gain their confidence back and helps increase their courage. This stone can also be used to diffuse anger and helps if you have gone through emotional abuse.

6. **Spiritual Uses**

Carnelian is known as a protector and can help bring balance to your chakras. It has also been known to benefit people to enhance their appreciation for life. On top of those benefits, carnelian can also help bring serenity and may be able to help recall past life events.

Chalcedony

If you are looking for a crystal that helps promote peace and joy, Chalcedony is the right stone for you. This is made out of a group of cryptocrystalline quartz minerals that form masses. There is a variety of this stone that comes in a wide array of colors. This crystal has the ability to relieve negative emotions and promotes overall happiness. Chalcedony is often referred to as the stone of brotherhood as it can promote group stability.

1. **Chakra**

Varies depending on the color

2. **Color**

White, Gray, Blue

3. **Rarity**

Common

4. **Physical Uses**

The most common use for this stone is to help balance and restore energy. It has also been known to help with nightmares, night terrors, and Alzheimer's disease.

5. **Emotional Uses**

Chalcedony is an excellent stone if you are looking to enhance your happiness in life. It has the ability to increase self-worth, self-confidence, and your emotional balance. This stone is also beneficial if you are looking to cope with grief or release negativity from your life. You may find that it brings you a sense of peace and has a calming effect.

Citrine

Citrine is another fairly popular stone as it has a very joyful vibration that has the ability to transmit its energies to those who surround it. This is very popular if you have suppressed anger or suffer from depression. Citrine is known to help increase optimism and will bring a more positive conscious mind over time. It is thought that this crystal is powered by the sun, which is why it has the ability to energize and cleanse the soul. If you are looking to cleanse your chakras, this crystal will benefit you most.

1. **Chakra**
   Sacral Chakra

2. **Color**
   Yellow

3. **Rarity**
   Common

4. **Physical Uses**
   Citrine has many wonderful benefits when it comes to physical ailments. It can help with verbal communication, tissue health, thyroid balance, spleen disorders, seasonal disorders, pancreas health, kidney disorders, headaches, food poisoning, eye disorders, digestive health, diabetes, and circulatory problems.

5. **Emotional Uses**
   If you have been having suicidal thoughts, citrine will be a must have for your collection. It can also help boost self-confidence, self-worth, and give you the hope you've been searching for in your life. The stone has also been known to increase courage, enjoyment, honestly, and even hope. If

you are looking to boost your creative expression, this may work for you as well.

6. Spiritual Uses

Citrine is great if you are looking to reduce the negative energy in your life. It also has the ability to help activate will and increase some individual's psychic abilities. Citrine can also be used to maximize your energy flow and can help ease phobias.

Clear Quartz

You have seen clear quartz mentioned several times throughout this book. It is one of the most popular and most versatile healing stones out there. This is due to its powerful healing nature and ability to work with just about any condition. Clear Quartz is a power stone and has the ability to boost energy and intention. It can also help individuals attune to their higher self, reduce negativity, and can relieve pain.

1. Chakra

Clear Quartz can work on all chakras.

2. Color

Clear

3. Rarity

Common

4. Physical Uses

As I mentioned earlier, clear quartz is very versatile. It can be beneficial for physical ailments such as vitality, vertigo, thyroid issues, sleep issues, post-surgery healing, pain relief, memory health, kidney disorders, immune system problems, heartburn, dental pain, burns, and problems associated with AIDS and HIV.

5. Emotional Uses

Clear Quartz is commonly used to help reduce tension and stress. It is also excellent for emotional balancing, healing, and stabilizing. This stone has also been known to help create joy, harmony, and acceptance in people's lives.

6. Spiritual Uses
Clear Quartz is great for spiritual uses. It can help with a number of issues including unity, telepathy, spiritual guidance and awakening, increases consciousness, creates connection to your Divine, connection with your inner child, communicating with spirit guides, communicating with angels, and can help with affirmation.

Danburite

As of today, danburite is one of the highest vibration minerals found. This crystal has the ability to connect the heart of your mind with the mind of your heart. This stone is highly sought after due to having high spiritual properties and is very powerful with the heart chakra. Danburite has the ability to work with your heart chakra to relieve emotional pain and increase the self. It is most commonly known to help an individual's true light shine through. It is very popular due to having gentle energy that is still fairly powerful. If you are going through a time of extreme change, danburite will be an excellent crystal to have with you to help ease the transition.

1. Chakra
Heart Chakra and Crown Chakra

2. Color
Clear

3. Rarity
Common

4. Physical Uses
Danburite is used to help several physical ailments. It can be used for tumors, tissue health, muscular issues, liver disorders, infertility, gallbladder problems, body weight management, body detox, and allergies.

5. Emotional Uses
This stone helps individuals open and revitalize their auras. It can also reduce stress, tension, and increase your sense of belonging with friends and family. As I mentioned earlier, it

is also excellent to help cope with extreme changes in your life.

6. **Spiritual Uses**

   Danburite is an extremely spiritual stone. It can help with a number of spiritual journeys such as truth-seeking, reiki, psychic work, spiritual work, protection, and can help some people communicate with angels. It is also popular with enhancing an individual's intuition and can protect you as well.

Dioptase

If you are searching for a stone that can help you relax and relieve mental stress, dioptase will be a great addition to your crystal collection. This stone has the ability to stimulate and clear all of your chakras so that you will be able to enter a higher level of awareness and bring refreshing energy to your body and soul. Dioptase is also beneficial if you are looking to further your spiritual attunement as it has the ability to stimulate your past life memories and promotes prosperity.

1. **Chakra**
   Heart Chakra

2. **Color**
   Turquoise or Green

3. **Rarity**
   Uncommon

4. **Physical Uses**
   Dioptase can help with several physical ailments. The powers of this stone can help with tumors, removing toxins, PMS symptoms, pain relief, muscle pain, lung problems, liver disorders, heartburn, heart problems, headaches, chronic pain, cancer, blood pressure issues, and abrasions.

5. **Emotional and Spiritual Uses**
   Dioptase is often used to help ease depression and balance your emotions. It is also beneficial if you are looking to reduce stress and create a sense of tranquility in your life.

On top of these benefits, it can also help you clear and cleanse your aura.

Emerald

Emerald is mostly associated with the Heart Chakra. This crystal is mostly used to enhance wisdom, unity, loyalty, and love for peoples' lives. When you use emerald on a group of people, it has been known to encourage bonding and increase both understanding and communication. On top of these amazing benefits, emerald is also useful if you are looking for mental clarity and enhance memory. If you are looking to connect to Divine Love, you can use the crystal in meditation to help you open your heart and accept all things.

1. **Chakra**
   Heart Chakra

2. **Color**
   Green

3. **Rarity**
   Common

4. **Physical Uses**
   Emerald is an excellent stone to use for a number of physical ailments. These can include overall weakness, vomiting, ulcers, nausea, memory health, liver disorders, immune system problems, heart issues, fever, infections, eye problems, colds, cancer, blood pressure, and arthritis.

5. **Emotional and Spiritual Uses**
   This stone is mostly used to help individuals calm down and creates a sense of tranquility in your life. It also has the ability to inspire some people and creates a sense of serenity and compassion. Emerald has also been known to help people cope with grief and gives them a sense of clarity.

Epidote

Epidote has the ability to enhance the energy of whatever this stone touches, this includes other stones which is why it is so popular. If you have other energies you are looking to enhance, you will need to add epidote to your crystal collection. This stone is excellent for releasing negative energy and increasing the perception of spiritual beings. It can also restore one's sense of optimism and can clear energy blockages.

1. **Chakra**
   Heart Chakra

2. **Color**
   Green

3. **Rarity**
   Common

4. **Physical Uses**
   Epidote can help with several physical ailments. Some of the more popular issues this stone can help include physical strength and recovery, vitamin absorption, kidney issues, weak immune systems, dehydration, and brain disorders.

5. **Emotional and Spiritual Uses**
   This stone is beneficial in several ways. For one, it has the ability to increase an individual's self-worth and self-confidence. It is also helpful if you are looking to ease depression. On the spiritual side, epidote is helpful if you are looking to raise vibrations and create a balance in your chakras.

Fluorite

Fluorite is another crystal that is fairly popular in the crystal healing world. This stone is very protective and is useful if you are looking to ground yourself. Mostly, this crystal works with your upper chakras and can help connect your mind to the universal consciousness. It also has the ability to clear your aura of energies that may be dragging you down.

Fluorite comes in several different colors. One example of this would be green fluorite. This version has the ability to access intuition. It can ground you and absorb any excess energy you may have. Use green fluorite if you wish to renew and cleanse your chakras.

Another popular version of fluorite is blue fluorite. The blue color helps clear communication between your physical and spiritual planes. This crystal is used to create a sense of serenity and calmness to help bring you inner peace.

1. **Chakra**
   Varies depending on the color

2. **Color**
   Purple, Green, Clear, and Blue

3. **Rarity**
   Common

4. **Physical Uses**
   Depending on the color of the fluorite you buy, it will have different physical benefits. This crystal can help with issues such as viruses, ulcers, spleen issues, sinus problems, pneumonia, physical coordination, pain relief, nutrition problems, vitamin absorption, muscle toning, memory health, lung problems, kidney issues, herpes, health, gallbladder problems, eating disorders, dental problems, broken bones, bone strengthening, bone disorders, arthritis, and issues with ADD and ADHD.

5. **Emotional and Spiritual Uses**
   Fluorite is a great stone to have if you are looking to balance your emotions. The power of the stone grants the ability to release any negativity or denial you may be holding onto. It can also help with healing and enhancing your intuition.

Fuchsite

This is the mineral of renewal and rejuvenation. Fuchsite is a stone that helps bring out your inner child and often sparks joy. It is a wonderful reminder that no matter how old we get, your heart and soul have an attitude of its own. Fuchsite can assist in clearing your consciousness and creates a balance in your mental and emotional states. This stone also has the ability to increase energy when combined with other crystals. If you are a healer, this will be a wonderful addition to your collection.

1. **Chakra**
   Heart Chakra and Throat Chakra

2. **Color**
   Green

3. **Rarity**
   Common

4. **Physical Uses**
   Fuchsite is an excellent stone to help with several physical ailments. It can help with issues of the throat, spine, snoring, larynx issues, inflammation, immune system problems, eczema, cellular disorders, and carpal tunnel problems.

5. **Emotional and Spiritual Uses**
   As mentioned, fuchsite is excellent to strengthen your emotional balances while bringing you both fun and joy. It also grants the ability to connect with angels and connect with the nature around you.

Garnet

Garnet is a popular crystal to have as it can help inspire a sense of brightness and light in your life. This is especially helpful if you are looking to help with depression or simply bring more joy back into your life. The crystal is also beneficial to help release the anger that you may be holding onto, especially if that anger is targeted at yourself. The fire of Garnet is known to bring courage and willpower to those who hold it in their hands. It can even "light a fire" under you to help you bring feelings to the surface. If the Garnet is powerful, it is also known to clean chakras of negative energies so that you can re-energize them.

1. **Chakra**
   Root Chakra, Heart Chakra, and Sacral Chakra.

2. **Color**
   Red

3. **Rarity**
   Common

4. **Physical Uses**
   Garnet is a crystal that can help with a number of physical ailments. Some of these issues include vitality, thyroid health, stomach problems diarrhea, constipation, pancreas health, pituitary gland issues, menopause, low blood pressure, libido, leg problems, kidney disorders, intestinal disorders, hyperactivity, heart issues, fatigue, exhaustion, colic, blood disorders, blood detoxing, blood circulation, arthritis, anemia, and abdominal pain.

5. **Emotional Uses**
   This crystal can also bring several benefits to your life on an emotional level. Garnet can help increase self-confidence, willpower, and self-worth. It has also been known to help with emotional issues that are involved with relationships, love, and loyalty to others. On top of these benefits, the stone may be able to increase your compassion as well.

6. **Spiritual Uses**
   Garnet is known to help people prosper and transform into the person they are meant to be. It can also be used to help create unity in your life as well as manifestation. Garnet can also come in a green color that helps people express themselves in situations where they are fearful to do so.

Halite

You may have heard of halite before as it is more commonly known as rock salt. This salt is mined in the Khewra Salt mines, which is one of the biggest salt mines in the world. While many of us typically use table salt, halite can be beneficial in your diet. This stone has the ability to cleanse your aura and can help deflect any negative energy in your life. Halite also has purification properties and is often kept in a bowl to rid of negative energies in a room. There are also halite salt lamps to help clear indoor pollutants.

1. **Chakra**
   Heart Chakra and Sacral Chakra

2. **Color**
   White, Pink, and Peach

3. **Rarity**
   Very Common

4. **Physical Uses**
   Halite has wonderful benefits for a number of popular ailments. One of the major reasons to introduce this stone into your home is to help with Seasonal Affective Disorder. It can also help with your nervous system, lung problems, infections, headache relief, migraine relief, chemical imbalance, fevers, asthma, and allergies.

5. **Emotional and Spiritual Uses**
   If you find yourself lacking self-confidence or self-worth, halite may be beneficial for you. It can also help with judgment and worrying. On top of these wonderful benefits, halite also can help you remove energy blocks and balance your aura.

Hematite

If you are looking for a crystal that has the ability to absorb negative energy and bring stress relief into your life, hematite will be an excellent option for you. This stone is protective and can help individuals stay grounded in a number of different situations. It is also beneficial if you want to work with your root chakra to help change your negative energy into positive vibrations. You can carry this stone with you if you need equilibrium or balance in your life. It is also beneficial if you need help focusing.

Please take note that when hematite is in its natural state, it has a slight magnetic charge. If you have a pacemaker, you will want to consult with your doctor before working with this stone. If a stone is marked Magnetic Hematite, it should be avoided if you have a pacemaker.

1. **Chakra**
   Root Chakra

2. **Color**

Silver and Metallic Gray

3. Rarity
Common

4. Physical Uses
Hematite is a wonderful stone to add to your collection as it can be used on a wide variety of physical ailments. Some of these include issues with yin and yang energy, weakness, tissue healing, smoking addiction, physical strength, pain relief, nutrient absorption, nose bleeds, nervous disorders, multiple-sclerosis, cramps, menstruation, leg cramps, kidney disorders, inflammation, insomnia, high blood pressure, focus, detoxifying, circulatory issues, broken bones, blood clotting problems, blood detoxing, back issues, anemia, and other addiction problems.

5. Emotional Uses
If you are looking to diffuse anger or release it from yourself, hematite can help you with this. It can also help balance your emotions as well as increase your self-worth and your self-confidence. This stone also has the ability to dispel any negativity in your life as well.

6. Spiritual Uses
As you start your crystal collection, you will want to have a spiritual protector. Hematite has the ability to protect you while also creating a sense of balance and harmony in your life. This stone will help bring awareness to the world around you and will also help to ground you through your life.

Howlite

Howlite is a popular crystal as it is an attunement stone. This means that it has the ability to connect you to higher spiritual consciousness. The stone will help prepare and open your mind to receive the wisdom of the attunements and the energy it provides. Howlite can also help if you experience stress, tension, and anxiety on a daily basis. By eliminating these stressors, it can help encourage the emotional expression of any individuals and help soothe them.

1. **Chakra**
   All Chakras but primarily the crown chakra

2. **Color**
   White

3. **Rarity**
   Common

4. **Physical Uses**
   Howlite is beneficial for several physical ailments. It can help with skeletal system problems, osteoporosis, lactating, dental issues, and bone disorders.

5. **Emotional Uses**
   This stone is used more for its emotional benefits. It can help diffuse any rage you may have and helps release anger you are holding onto. Howlite can also be beneficial to calm yourself and creates a higher sense of creative expression in some individuals. It has also been known to help people become unselfish as well.

6. **Spiritual Uses**
   Howlite has several spiritual benefits aside from helping people clear and cleanse their aura. It can also help maximize your energy flow and connects you to spirit guides. Some people also use howlite to help recall past life events.

Jadeite

Jadeite is the second member of the jade family. This stone is known as the stone of harmony and can help bring people together in a group setting. This is an excellent crystal to have if you are looking to strengthen the relationships between friends, family, or even business colleagues. This stone also works if you are looking to fix a relationship that was torn apart due to a loss or separation. Jadeite is also extremely helpful for children who are dealing with changing hormones or feel alone.

1. **Chakra**
   Heart Chakra and Root Chakra

2. Color
Yellow, White, Red, Pink, Orange, Lavender, Green, Blue, and Black

3. Rarity
Fairly Common

4. Physical Uses
Jadeite is beneficial for several physical issues. These can include skin infections, issues with reproductive organs, cramps, cellular disorders, bone disorders, and blood pressure regulation.

5. Emotional and Spiritual Uses
If you are looking to enhance and recall lucid dreaming, jadeite will be a must-have for your crystal collection. It can also help with love and all different kinds of relationships. Jadeite has the ability to create harmony in people's lives and can help with abundance and prosperity for some.

Kyanite

Specifically, we will be discussing black kyanite. This stone helps with clairvoyance and the manifestation of vision. This stone is a favorite among healers as it is full of healing energy and is helpful in healing any of the chakras. Kyanite helps send energy to any holes or tears that exist in your chakras and can help sweep away any negative energy you may be experiencing.

Black Kyanite is also beneficial if you are looking to open communication between people. With this, it is also used to ground individuals while their chakras are being aligned. It is popular to use while healing because it has the ability to heal and energize at the same time and makes for a wonderful meditation tool.

Overall, this stone has the ability to amplify energy, making it a wonderful tool for attunements as well. Kyanite may help bring tranquility to your life and can calm you for meditation.

1. **Chakra**
   Root Chakra

2. **Color**
   Black, Blue, Green, Orange

3. **Rarity**
   Common

4. **Emotional Uses**
   Kyanite is a popular stone to use when looking to enhance communication and expression. It is also beneficial if you are looking to get in touch with your creative expression. With these benefits, the crystal carries a calming effect that people are often searching for when they are trying to heal themselves.

5. **Spiritual Uses**
   Kyanite is mostly used for spiritual benefits. It can help with several spiritual issues such as spiritual protection, vision quests, recalling past life events, dream recalling and interpretation, clairvoyance, balancing the chakras, and also helps with attunements.

Labradorite

Labradorite is thought to be highly mystical. It is a crystalline form of Feldspar but is widely known for its flash when it catches the light. This stone is wonderful to heighten your intuition and also has the ability to enhance psychic abilities. Many people use labradorite to work with their third eye chakra because it is able to balance both intellect and intuition. On top of these wonderful benefits, the stone can also protect individuals from negative energies while balancing their strength and aura from any energy leaks at the same time.

1. **Chakra**
   Third Eye Chakra and Crown Chakra

2. **Color**
   Iridescent

3. **Rarity**
   Common

4. **Physical Uses**
   Labradorite has the ability to help people with a number of different physical ailments. Some of these problems could be stomach issues, diarrhea, constipation, addiction to smoking, certain skin infections, seizures, can boost metabolism, helps with eye disorders, emphysema, brain disorders, and other addictions.

5. **Emotional Uses**
   If you are looking to increase your self-confidence or your self-worth, labradorite may be beneficial for you. This stone also has the ability to enhance codependence if that is something you need to work on.

6. **Spiritual Uses**
   Labradorite is a very spiritual stone and can be beneficial for a number of spiritual ailments. As mentioned earlier, this stone is mostly used to help balance the third chakra. On top of this benefit, it can also help with telepathy, psychic attacks, personal empowerment, mediumship, meditation, stimulating and enhancing creams, cosmic awareness, consciousness, communication with spirits, communication with the higher self, clairvoyance, helps to protect the aura, cleans the aura, and can help with the ascension process.

Lapis Lazuli

This stone is made of a combination of several different minerals. These minerals include Lazurite, Pyrite, and Calcite. It is believed that Lapis Lazuli has existed since the birth of time and was used by ancient Hebrews. This is why the stone is best known for the power of spoken words. If you are looking to open and balance your throat chakras, Lapis Lazuli can help you with verbal expression.

Lapis Lazuli also has the ability to open the third eye chakra. It is thought that this stone can connect to the celestial and physical kingdoms. This stone is very peaceful and can connect with physical guardians. It is also known to help shield individuals from negative energy and can protect against psychic attacks.

1. **Chakra**
   Throat Chakra and Third Eye Chakra

2. **Color**
   Indigo

3. **Rarity**
   Common

4. **Physical Uses**
   Lapis Lazuli is used for many different physical ailments. Some of the more popular problems it can help with include vomiting, vertigo, throat issues, sleep apnea, shingles, pregnancy problems, panic attacks, pain, menstrual cramps, menopause, laryngitis, insomnia, immune system support, herpes, hearing issues, migraine and headache relief, fainting, eye disorders, epilepsy, ear infections, dizziness, dental issues, cramps, coma, chronic pain, brain disorders, problems with bone marrow, bone disorders, body detox, birthing problems, birthing pains, asthma, and other aches and pains.

5. **Emotional Uses**
   As for emotional uses, this stone also carries many benefits for a number of ailments. Some of these problems can include issues with self-worth and self-confidence, suicidal thoughts, reduces stress, helps with panics attacks and perseverance, helps with obsessive-compulsive disorder, melancholy, hope, emotional healing, emotional abuse, helps with criticism, grief, calming, and overall anxiety.

6. **Spiritual Uses**
   As mentioned, Lapis Lazuli is mostly used to help balance the third eye chakra. It can also help with spiritual protection, spiritually uplifting, psychic protection, psychic attacks, reincarnation, meditation, and karma. It is also known to help enhance intuition, psychic abilities, and the

ability to spirits. Lapis Lazuli may also help with balancing your aura.

Malachite

This stone is one of the more popular healing crystals as it has the ability to absorb energy and helps draw certain emotions to the surface. Malachite is known as the stone of intention, manifestation, abundance, and balance. It can help you clear your chakra and stimulate them. This stone is mostly used to clean energy and bring positive transformation to those who use it. Due to Malachite's ability to amplify all types of energies, it is recommended you use this stone in small doses.

1. **Chakra**
   Heart Chakra

2. **Color**
   Green

3. **Rarity**
   Common

4. **Physical Uses**
   Malachite is known to help with several physical ailments. Some of these issues include tumor growths, vertigo, toxins, skin infections, scoliosis, radiation, post-surgery healing, pancreas health, pain relief, muscular issues, muscle pain, liver disorders, joint pain, inflammation, infertility, immune system issues, healing, headaches, migraines, dizziness, dental pain, congestion, colic, chemotherapy, cancer, bone disorders, body detox, birthing issues, viral infections, back problems, asthma, and arthritis.

5. **Emotional Uses**
   With physical benefits, malachite can also help with several emotional ailments. If you feel your emotions are out of whack, this stone can help you remove any blockages you may have so you can restore your emotional energy. This stone can also help increase self-confidence, self-worth, and hope in your life. It has also been known to help shy individuals be able to express themselves.

6. Spiritual Uses
As mentioned, this stone is mostly used to help with the heart chakra. It can also help absorb energy and protect your spirit.

Moonstone

As you can probably already tell, moonstone is associated with the moon and can help people connect to the Goddess within them. This stone is best known for its ability to balance the emotional body and helps individuals connect to their intuition. Moonstone is best for those who typically have an aggressive personality as it helps relieve stress and can also offer protective energies.

1. Chakra
Sacral Chakra, Crown Chakra, Third Eye Chakra

2. Color
White, Tan, and Cream

3. Rarity
Common

4. Physical Uses
Moonstone has some wonderful physical benefits. Some of the more common issues that it can help with includes water retention, vomiting, stomach issues, pregnancy, PMS, pituitary gland problems, muscular and skeletal issues, multiple sclerosis, menstrual cramps, menstruation, insomnia, insect bites, infertility, health, headache relief, edema, circulatory problems, breast health, birthing issues, and arthritis.

5. Emotional Uses
Moonstone offers some emotional benefits alongside the physical benefits as well. It has the ability to help with postpartum depression, enhances positive energy, can help with letting go, mood swings, fear of the dark, emotional healing, emotional balancing, happiness, centering, composure, and also helps release anger.

6. Spiritual Uses

Sometimes, we suffer from spiritual ailments. Moonstone can help with spiritual protection, visual quests, stimulating and enhancing dreams, enhancing intuition, and can help individuals connect to a higher realm. It is also known to increase ancient wisdom and bring awareness back into your life. If you are looking to revitalize and balance your aura, moonstone can help with this too.

Obsidian

While there are a few different versions of obsidian, we are going to focus on black obsidian. Oftentimes, it is referred to as the wizard stone as it is thought to have magical problems. In the modern world, many people choose to wear this stone to help protect them against hostile environments, stress, and negative energy. It can also be used as décor in your home to help protect you against electromagnetic fields.

1. Chakra
Root Chakra

2. Color
Black

3. Rarity
Common

4. Physical Uses
Mostly, obsidian is helpful for physical protection and pain relief. It may also be able to help with physical ailments such as knee pain, joint pain, circulatory problems, blockages, and arthritis.

5. Emotional and Spiritual Uses
Obsidian is a beneficial crystal to have if you are looking to release any stress or emotional blockages you may be suffering from. It is also great if you need positive energy in your life or helps to ground yourself. This crystal also has the ability to protect you against psychic attacks.

Onyx

Onyx is a powerful protection stone that has the ability to absorb and transform any negative energy in your life. This is important as negative energy often drains our personal energy. By getting rid of the negativity, you may find that your physical and emotional strength will increase as you become less stressed.

This stone also encourages good fortune and happiness, helping people heal from past life issues they may be holding onto. On top of this benefit, many people use black onyx while they are dreaming or meditating to help ground themselves.

1. **Chakra**
   Root Chakra

2. **Color**
   Black

3. **Rarity**
   Common

4. **Physical Uses**
   Onyx is beneficial for several physical issues. Some of these ailments include ovarian disorders, obesity, birthing problems, allergies, alcoholism, and other addictions.

5. **Emotional and Spiritual Uses**
   This stone is excellent if you are looking to reduce or release any negative energy in your life. It also has the ability to soothe the soul and can help people who have anxiety. On top of these benefits, onyx is also known to help ground individuals when they need it most.

Peridot

Peridot is a crystal that helps bring positive energy to those going through traumatic situations and is highly vibrational with your heart chakra. This stone also has the power to bring out unconditional love for those who seek it and can help with several relationship roles. For this reason, peridot is often worn during social interactions.

1. **Chakra**
   Heart Chakra and Solar Plexus Chakra

2. **Color**
   Green

3. **Rarity**
   Common

4. **Physical Uses**
   Peridot has the ability to work with a wide range of physical ailments. Some of the more common treatments can be for trauma, tissue healing, thyroid balance, spleen issues, smoking addiction, muscle toning, lungs, liver disorders, intestinal issues, indigestion, heartburn, eye infections, breast health, blood sugar regulation, and birthing problems.

5. **Emotional Uses**
   This crystal is most commonly used for emotional benefits. Peridot can help with resentment, reduces stress and tension, diffuses rage, lessens jealousy, decreases irritability, can ease depression, help cope with grief, and is found to be a very comforting healing stone. This stone can also be used to help with emotional abuse and emotional healing.

6. **Spiritual Uses**
   Peridot has been known to have several spiritual benefits as well. It can be used to stimulate spiritual insight, enhances creative expression, can cleanse the aura, and may even help in vision quests.

Rose Quartz

As you may have already guessed, rose quartz is one of the most popular healing crystals. This stone is the stone of unconditional love and works with the heart chakra to help open your heart to all different kinds of love. Whether you are seeking the love of family, romantic love, or even the love of friends, the high energy of this stone can help you.

Rose Quartz also has soothing energy. It helps many people foster emotions of forgiveness, reconciliation, and empathy toward others. While lowering your stress levels, this stone can help clear any resentment, jealousy, or anger you are harnessing toward others. Instead, you will attract love through the romance stone and help yourself express feelings you may be keeping bottled up inside.

1. **Chakra**
   Heart Chakra

2. **Color**
   Pink

3. **Rarity**
   Common

4. **Physical Uses**
   Rose Quartz may be able to help you with a number of physical problems. Some issues include skin infections, shingles, PTSD, pain relief, neck problems, menstrual cramps, lung issues, kidney disorders, infertility, headache relief, fatigue, eating disorders, dying process, dementia, coughing, burns, bruising, and Alzheimer's disease.

5. **Emotional Uses**
   This stone is excellent if you are looking for a healing stone to help with your emotions. Rose Quartz can help with all types of relationships, reduce stress, enhance love, decrease jealousy and guilt, decrease fear while increasing emotional strength, and helps some people cope with grief. If you are looking to diffuse anger and create a sense of calm for yourself, rose quartz can help with this too.

6. **Spiritual Uses**
   Rose Quartz is most commonly used to bring users unconditional love. It also can help with spiritual love, increases positive energy, and helps some people connect with the Christ consciousness. On top of this, the stone is also known to help connect with the divine love through the heart chakra.

Ruby

Are you looking to open your heart chakra? Ruby is a very powerful heart stone that can help protect against lost heart energy and can dissolve any emotional congestion you may have. This stone has the ability to balance and heal emotions involved with connecting to others. Ruby grants the ability to express love and facilitate new relationships.

1. **Chakra**
   Heart Chakra and Root Chakra

2. **Color**
   Red

3. **Rarity**
   Common

4. **Physical Uses**
   Ruby is a stone that is used often with a number of physical ailments. This stone can help with urinary tract issues, ulcers, stomach problems, skin infections, sexual abuse, pregnancy, reproductive organ issues, physical strength, night terrors, menstrual cramps, menopause, leg issues, kidney problems, intestinal disorders, infertility, heart problems, fever, brain disorders, bone disorders, blood pressure regulation, blood circulation problems, bleeding, anemia, and abrasions.

5. **Emotional Uses**
   Ruby is an excellent stone if you are looking to build your self-confidence and self-worth. It is also beneficial to gain courage, happiness, inspiration, and passion. If you are looking to balance and stabilize your emotion, this will be an excellent addition to your crystal collection.

6. Spiritual Uses
Ruby is also beneficial for spiritual uses. This stone is known to help reduce negative energy and has the ability to create long distance healing. If you are looking to work with your heart chakra or strengthen your aura, ruby may be able to work for you as well.

Sapphire

Sapphire is most popularly known as a stone of tranquility, peace, and spiritual truth. If you are looking to channel healing energies from a higher source, this is an excellent stone to add to your collection, especially if you practice Reiki. Sapphire has the ability to guide users on the spiritual path and can help boost both spiritual and psychic powers.

I mentioned earlier that there are Biblical references of Sapphire being placed in the breastplate of High Priests. It is believed that this stone has protective powers and seems to have been used through history. There are many different colors of sapphire depending on the trace metals they have.

1. Chakra
Throat Chakra, Crown Chakra, and Third Eye Chakra

2. Color
Purple, Pink, and Blue

3. Rarity
Common

4. Physical Uses
Sapphire can help with several physical ailments. Some believe it helps with tumors, nausea, motion sickness, hearing problems, eye disorders, eczema, brain disorders, and altitude sickness.

5. Emotional and Spiritual Uses
Sapphire is beneficial for a number of emotional and spiritual issues. It helps many bring happiness, hope, and wisdom back into their lives. It also has a calming effect that helps many individuals release negative energy they are

holding onto. Sapphire is also thought to help some people communicate with spirits and can be beneficial to use during meditation.

Smoky Quartz

Throughout this book, you have seen smoky quartz mentioned several times. This is a very powerful stone and emits high levels of energy. Mostly, smoky quartz is used to ground people and is used to work with both the solar plexus chakra and the root chakra. This stone can be highly beneficial because it has the ability to transmute and absorb negative energy. It also provides relief and can help after a strong energy session. The best part of this stone is the fact that the energy is slow and steady but still powerful. It has the ability to help you transform your dreams into reality.

1. **Chakra**
   Root Chakra

2. **Color**
   Brown

3. **Rarity**
   Common

4. **Physical Uses**
   Smoky Quartz is popular for a number of physical ailments. It can help with understanding death, tumor growth, skin infections, toxin removal, radiation, pancreas issues, pain relief, night terrors, nightmares, kidney issues, infertility, headaches, migraines, foot problems, chemotherapy, cancer, balancing issues, and abdominal problems.

5. **Emotional Uses**
   This stone can also benefit users if they are having emotional problems. It can help ease any stress or tension in your life. Smoky quartz is also beneficial to ground individuals and helps ease depression. If you are holding onto resentment toward another individual, it can also help with that.

6. **Spiritual Use**

Smoky Quartz is a powerful spiritual healing stone. It can help with the root chakra and has the ability to help individuals release and dispel any negativity they are holding onto. It is also thought to have psychic protection and can help individuals cleanse and clear their aura. Smoky Quartz is beneficial in the home as well as it can protect people from pollutions, smog, and electromagnetic frequencies.

Tiger Eye

While there are several different versions of Tiger's Eye, we will be focusing on golden or brown tiger eye. This stone has the ability to draw spiritual energy to the earth. Golden Tiger Eye specifically has the power to bring optimism and brightness into your life, while shining light on any issues you may be having. It is also widely known to protect travelers and can bring individuals good luck.

If you add this stone to your collection, it is great to carry around with you when you need help dealing with any issues that include concentration, control, will, or power. It is also beneficial for those looking to boost their creative energy. Overall, it works closely with your solar plexus chakra to help increase your power.

1. **Chakra**
   Solar Plexus Chakra, Sacral Chakra, and Third Eye Chakra

2. **Color**
   Yellow and Gold

3. **Rarity**
   Common

4. **Physical Uses**
   Tiger Eye can be beneficial for a number of physical ailments. It has been known to help with the throat, reproductive organs, mental diseases, hepatitis, gallbladder problems, fatigue, eye disorders, bone disorders, and balance problems.

5. **Emotional Uses**

This stone is excellent to work with your emotions thanks to its ability to ground users. It can help with self-criticism, self-confidence, pride, personality disorders, goals, depression, creative expression, coping with change, commitment problems, and balancing problems.

6. **Spiritual Uses**
   It is believed that Tiger Eye can help enhance psychic ability. It is also known to increase spiritual protection and creates a sense of balance. Some also believe that Tiger's Eye can help some communicate with animals!

Tourmaline

Tourmaline is a popular crystal used in metaphysical circles. It is believed that this stone has the ability to balance the brain, clear energy blockages, and can transmute any negative energy you may have. It is also beneficial as a healer and a protector stone by boosting sympathy, empathy, and compassion.

1. **Chakra**
   Dependent on Color

2. **Color**
   Pink, Green, Clear, Brown, Blue, and Black

3. **Rarity**
   Common

4. **Physical Uses**
   This stone can help with some physical uses. Some ailments tourmaline can benefit include tonsillitis, the sense of taste and smell, muscular problems, muscle pain, lymphatic system issues, low blood pressure, indigestion, immune support, hearing issues, epilepsy, cancer, anemia, and abrasions.

5. **Emotional and Spiritual Uses**
   Tourmaline is known to help with several emotional and spiritual ailments. This stone can help bring peace, happiness, and harmony back into your life. It is also popularly used to cleanse auras and balance masculine

energy. On top of these wonderful benefits, tourmaline also has the ability to help people cope with grief and bring courage back into their life. This is especially true for those looking to stabilize their emotions after going through specific types of abuse.

Turquoise

Turquoise is believed to be the bridge between heaven and earth. Several cultures believe this stone has the ability to connect our minds to the universe. This may be why it is so popular in jewelry all around the world. Turquoise has wonderful benefits including releasing and removing any old behaviors you may have such as self-sabotage.

This stone works closely with the throat chakra, granting people the ability to speak honestly and clearly, especially in public. With turquoise, you may find you have the ability to express yourself freely while the stone provides you with both strength and purification of your heart and soul.

1. **Chakra**
   Throat Chakra

2. **Color**
   Green-Blue, Sky Blue, Green, and Blue

3. **Rarity**
   Common

4. **Physical Uses**
   Turquoise can be used for several different ailments. These include rheumatism, pain relief, nutrient absorption, night terrors, nightmares, muscle pain, lung problems, infection, healing, migraine relief, eye disorders, breathing issues, and blood oxygenation.

5. **Emotional and Spiritual Uses**
   Mostly, turquoise is used to bring peace and kindness into people's lives. It can also help promote empathy and friendship for other people. Turquoise has wonderful

benefits with mental clarity and public speaking if that is something you have trouble with.

Zircon

Finally, we end with zircon as crystals you should consider for your collection. For a very long time, zircon has been known as a protective stone. Depending on the color of the stone, it has the ability to renew your sense of joy and enthusiasm for life. It also helps some people to bring peace into their life after they have gone through a traumatic event.

It should be noted that if you have epilepsy or wear a pacemaker, you should not wear Zircon. Some people have noted that this stone can cause dizziness if you have either of these ailments.

1. **Chakra**
   Root Chakra

2. **Color**
   Yellow, Grey, Green, Copper, Clear, Brown, Black

3. **Rarity**
   Fairly Common

4. **Physical Uses**
   Zircon can benefit some specific physical ailments. Most commonly, it is used for viruses, vertigo, ulcers, sexually transmitted diseases, poison, muscle pain, insomnia, brain disorders, bone disorders, and allergies.

5. **Emotional and Spiritual Uses**
   If you are looking to clear and cleanse your aura, zircon may be beneficial for your collection. It is also known to bring an individual's vitality, protection, and joy!

CHAPTER FIVE

Other Uses For Crystals

With all of these incredible healing benefits crystals can bring into your life, it may be hard to believe that people use crystals for anything else! Indeed, crystals can have several roles in your life. Some other uses for crystals include energizing, grounding, meditating, decorating, and more! In the chapter to follow, we will be going over just some of the other ways you can use your crystal collection.

Energizing

As we go through our day, sometimes, we need a little boost of energy. There are energizing stones that can help you get through tough times when you are feeling weak or fatigued. It should be noted that these types of crystals have higher vibrations and should be used sparingly. If you are looking to temper the healing crystal, try wrapping them in gold. You can also keep the crystals on your bedside if you are looking for a good night's rest. Two of the most popular energizing crystals include topaz and opal.

Grounding

You may not realize it just yet, but the ground beneath you is more important than you realize. Everyone needs to have solid ground beneath them to be the best version of themselves. A grounding stone will keep you from floating away or forgetting who you are. A powerful healing stone can help root you and bring awareness back into your life. Some popular grounding stones include smoky quartz, petrified wood, hematite, coral, and bloodstone.

Manifesting

Some people choose to have healing stones and crystals to help manifest certain powers. These stones can help you focus on the things in life you really want. They can also help you maintain a positive mindset when you need it most. Some of the more popular stones used for this purpose include onyx, sapphire, green quartz, bloodstone, and citrine.

You can also use manifesting stones to help during the meditation process. Stones such as alabaster, amethyst, and geode can help connect to your power source. If you need help focusing during meditation, try holding lapis, iolite, or lepidolite.

Record Keeping

In the crystal healing community, people believe that stones are both wise and ancient. Certain stones have the ability to absorb and retain memories. In general, it seems as thought red-colored stones are the best at holding onto information. If you are a student, stones such as ruby, garnet, or carnelian may be beneficial to carry with you to class. The stone can help you focus and stay grounded during lecture. It may also be beneficial to bring this memory-keeper with you to exam days for some extra help!

Protection and Shielding

As you have already learned throughout this book, healing crystals have certain energy shields that can help protect you. If you wear certain crystals, they can shield and absorb energies around you. Stones such as pyrite, yellow jasper, diamond, and fluorite can absorb bad vibrations around you, so you can remain happy and positive.

Love

If you are looking for love in your life, there are love stones you can add to your collection. These stones typically have warm and soft energies that can bring love into your life. Typically, the love stones attract love and help people learn how to love themselves. If you are looking to bring more compassion in your life, try kunzite, moonstone, morganite, rose quartz, or even apatite.

Enlightenment

These stones are known as seeker stones. Stones such as celestite, moldavite, topaz, and Tiger's Eye can help elevate energetic vibrations. If you are looking to gain knowledge from the astral plane or connect to your higher self, an enlightenment stone will be beneficial to add to your collection. Some other seeker stones include selenite, sodalite, and Sunstone.

Goddess Energy

Are you looking to increase your feminine energy? There are healing stones for that! You don't need to be female to seek feminine energy. Each and every person is a blend of both feminine and masculine aspects. If you are looking to soften yourself in a difficult situation, you can try any of the goddess energy stones like peridot, moonstone, or chrysocolla.

Decorating

Your home can mean a number of different things to you. Your home is your sacred space, your sanctuary, your safe haven, your personal space, and where your heart is. Oftentimes, we decorate our homes with different pieces of arts, plants, and items that are important to us. Some people choose to add crystals to their décor because not only do they look beautiful, they can also have healing effects too.

One of the more popular crystals to decorate with is black obsidian. This crystal is a glossy black color and is a very strong protection stone. Black obsidian has the ability to cleanse your house of negative energy, anger, fear, greed, or resentment. I suggest using this crystal in your study or TV room to help absorb any electromagnetic emissions from appliances in your home. You can also place it near your front door to help stop any negative energy from entering your home in the first place.

Another stone you can place at the front door to greet friends and family is rose quartz! This stone helps increase happiness and joy in a gentle and loving manner. If you are looking to increase love and friendship in your home, rose quartz will be an excellent addition.

Next, we have rock salt! This crystal is most beneficial in your kitchen. It can be used for cooking but also can be a symbol of hospitality and prosperity. Rock Salts have energy that helps clear away any negative energy you may have in your environment. It also helps promote family harmony and can be used to cleanse your energy.

Another room you may want to decorate in your house is the bathroom. With healing crystals, you can help make this space serene and relaxing. I suggest using amethyst or rose quartz to help cleanse your physical body of any negative emotions and create a serene and stress-free environment. You can even place these stones in the bath water with you when you aren't displaying them!

Finally, it is time to take a look at your bedroom. Many of us spend a lot of time in the bedroom and crystals can help depending on what your goal is. Before you decorate, you must first ask yourself what you want from the crystals. Are you looking to sleep better? Perhaps you are looking to increase your love and intimacy in the bedroom. Once you have your goal set, you can do some research to find the perfect crystal for your space.

One of the more classic crystal placements for this room is right under the mattress. Many people place three quartz crystals to help bring a protective and relaxing energy to your bed. This is perfect if you are looking to sleep better. You will want to be careful when selecting your crystals as some people are sensitive to the energy from crystals.

If you are looking to boost love in the bedroom, you will want to consider rose quartz. As you will recall, this is the stone for universal love. This stone can emit calming energy to help anyone in the room open their heart and remove negative energy. On top of having healing energy, rose quartz is also very pretty to look at. I suggest placing this stone in every corner of the room to benefit the most from the energy.

Of course, you are welcome to get as creative as you wish with crystals! These are just some suggestions if you are looking for other ways to use your collection. Now that you know all of the wonderful benefits that come with healing crystals, it is time to learn how to take care of them. In the chapter to follow, we will be going over how to cleanse and recharge your crystal, so you can continue to benefit from them!

CHAPTER SIX

How To Care For Crystals

As you begin to collect crystals, it will be important that you cleanse them on a regular basis. I highly suggest cleansing a crystal when you first receive it. You already know that crystals naturally absorb energy. When you cleanse the crystal, it can remove any energy it picked up before it landed in your hands. This will be especially important if you are planning on working energetically with crystals through meditation or healing work. If you do not cleanse your crystal when you first receive it, it could pass the energy from the last person onto you.

When Should I Clean My Crystal?

As you work more with crystals, you will have a better idea of when your crystals need to be cleansed. One crystal you can tell that needs cleaning is quartz crystals. This stone becomes cloudy and loses its luster when it needs to be cleansed. Other crystals will typically become heavier as they carry an extra load of energy.

If you have crystals you use around the house or wear on your person often, I suggest cleansing these on a more regular basis. You will know a crystal needs cleansing if you feel a lack of energy from them. Crystals such as quartz also need to be cleansed if you are planning on reprogramming the energy to benefit something new.

Methods of Cleansing Crystals

There are several different methods you can use to cleanse your crystals. As you work with healing crystals more, you will be able to find which works best for you. At the end of the day, you will want your crystals to be clear of all energy, so you can continue to use them.

The first method we will discuss is cleansing the crystals with your own energy. You will do this through intention and a focused mind. To cleanse the crystal with your energy, try holding the crystal in your hand and imagine immersing the crystal with a white light. This white light have the ability to clear any unwanted energy. It can also help re-energize the crystal as you hold it and ask the crystal to transform all of the energy into divine love and light.

Another method of cleaning crystal is through running water. It is believed that most crystals enjoy running water, so you can hold it under the tap and allow cold water to wash over it. As you do this, focus your mind on the crystals and visualize any negative energy within the crystal washing away and dissolving. This focus will help transform the energy into positive healing energy.

It should be noted that when you use water to cleanse your crystals, you will want it to be cold. You should never use hot or warm water to cleanse the stones. Please also understand that water is not recommended for all crystals. Some stones you will not want to use water include calcite, opals, turquoise, malachite, hanksite, celestite, or pearls. These stones have a composition that can be damaged by water. You will also want to use natural water as chlorine and other chemicals can also damage the crystals.

People have also been known to bathe their crystals in rainwater or water that comes from a natural source such as the river, ocean, or spring. If you soak in natural water, you will want to dry them in natural sunlight, too. Morning sunlight and moonlight allow light to filter through the crystal to help cleanse them. The best time to cleanse your crystal through moonlight is when you have a full moon.

Smoke is another popular method of cleaning crystal. You will want to use sacred herbs like lavender, cedar, or sage to cleanse the energetic matrix of your crystals. You can smudge with white sage if you are looking to remove negative energy. To smudge the crystals, you will light the herb, burn them, and when the flame dies, you can run the crystal through the smoke to help purify it.

The last two methods of cleansing crystals take a bit more time. One of these methods is to place the crystals on a rock salt bed for a day or two. This has been known to help max a crystal's energetic matrix. Another method is to bury the crystal in the earth for two to seven days. The longer you leave the crystals in, the deeper the cleanse will be. You will want to make sure you choose a safe location so that the crystals won't be lost or stolen. This method is a very slow but gentle way to cleanse your healing stones.

Methods of Recharging Crystals

Once you have cleansed your crystal, you will want to recharge them and renew their energy. There are a few different methods you can try. As you work with your crystal collection, you will be able to find a method that works best for them!

The first method of recharging crystal is through sunlight. You will want to place your crystals in the sunlight for an hour or two. You can place them on a windowsill or on the earth. Crystals can be charged under the stars, moon, or sun. The moon is typically a gentler method of recharging your crystals. A full moon is best for penetrating your crystals to recharge.

Another way of recharging your crystals is to place them in dynamic weather conditions. If you get a chance, try recharging your crystals in a thunderstorm. The energy from the storm can provide electromagnetic charge to your crystals, and you may feel the energy when you use them soon after the storm.

Crystal Storage

Crystals are very fragile and need to be treated carefully. Typically, crystals enjoy being out in the open so that they can work to their full potential, but if you need to store them, there are certain methods you can use to keep them safe and sound.

First, you will want to select a location that is dry and clean. If you choose an area that has a lot of moisture or dust, this can destroy or damage your crystal. One location for fragile crystals is a box. This can help keep your crystals protected from the environment.

If you have crystals that are smaller or more fragile, you will want to keep them in divided containers. While some people use egg cartons, others choose to invest in special crystal boxes. It is important to keep some crystals separate, so they don't damage softer materials. You can do this by lining your box with cotton balls or pads.

If you have polished crystals, you can keep them in a few different places. They typically do well in pockets, under pillows, or even in a bowl. How you store your crystals is ultimately up to you. Remember that each crystal is unique, and the energy of that crystal can never be replaced. These crystals are true gifts from the universe and should be taken care of as such.

CONCLUSION

I wish to thank you for reading through my book on healing crystals. I hope that you were able to find all of the information you were seeking and that I was able to provide you with the tools you need for your crystal healing journey. Now that you have been granted with all of this wonderful information, the next step is to try some of the techniques in your life and figure out which method works best for you. Remember that there truly are numerous benefits healing crystals can bring to you. It will take time and effort to build your own crystal collection, but you will find it will be worth it.

If you enjoyed this book, I would appreciate if you took the time to rate it on Amazon. Your honest review will be appreciated. I thank you for taking the time to learn from crystals and wish you the best of luck on your crystal healing journey. May you benefit from the healing powers and live your life to the fullest. Thank you!

DESCRIPTION

Are you looking to balance your body, mind, and soul? If so, there may be a healing crystal for you. Holistic healing methods can help bring positive energy into your life to help you become the best version of you! In this book, *Crystal Healing Bible: The Ultimate Guide to Gain Enlightenment and Awaken Your Energetic Potential with the Healing Powers of Crystals*, author Crystal Lee will walk you through everything you need to know to get you started on your healing journey.

This book will provide you with:

- Basics of Crystal Healing
- How to Start Your Own Crystal Collection
- Incredible Benefits of Crystal Healing
- Basics of Chakra Connections and Crystals
- Over 40 Crystals You Need to Know
- How to Harness the Power of Crystals
- And More!

If you suffer from issues such as trust, stress, self-confidence, rejection, regret, negativity, motivation, or love, there is a crystal for you. Start today and discover the incredible natural cures crystals can perform for you.